THE IMPORTANCE OF WAITING ON GOD

When Time and Testing Meets Maturity

KEVIN L. LIPSEY, SR. & STEPHANIE LIPSEY

THE IMPORTANCE OF WAITING ON GOD

When Time and Testing Meets Maturity

KEVIN L. LIPSEY, SR. & STEPHANIE LIPSEY

T&J Publishers
A Small Independent Publisher
with a Big Voice

Published by T&J Publishers (www.TandJPublishers.com)
Atlanta, GA.

Copyright © 2015 by Kevin L. Lipsey, Sr., and Stephanie S. Lipsey
Kevin L. Lipsey, Sr., Publisher / Editorial Director
Photography by Cornell McBride, Jr./McBride Creative
Poetry by Kevin L. Lipsey, Sr.
Book Cover and Formatting by Timothy Flemming, Jr.

All rights reserved. No part of this book may be reproduced or transmitted in any form or by any means—electronic or mechanical, including photocopying, recording or by any information storage and retrieved system without written permission from the authors, except for the inclusion of brief quotations in a review. The publication is sold with the understanding that the Publisher is not engaged in rendering legal or other professional services. If legal advice or other expert assistance is required, the services of a competent professional person should be sought.

Disclaimer: Any views or opinions presented in this book are solely those of the authors and are not meant to defame, insult or offend anyone. This book contains invaluable factual information and is intended only to minister to those who have been broken and are in need of understanding and encouragement. If you are not the envisioned recipient as previously stated, Kevin and Stephanie Lipsey accept no liability for the content of this book viewed in a derogatory manner aside from its intent of love and truth, or for the consequences of any actions taken on the basis of the information provided as the book or its content is not intended for you. It is our prayer that people are blessed through our real-life experiences, and know that you too, can make it through life's many problems with God's leading the way. May God Bless!

ISBN: 978-0-69253997-2
Library of Congress Control Number: 2015917289
klsrministries@gmail.com
www.KLMinistriesinc.com

DEDICATION

We would like to dedicate this book to Kiara, Chandler, Kevin, Jr., and Mya.
It is our prayer that you will reflect on these lessons of life and continue to grow in the grace of God.
You are the heartbeat of our heart…We love you always.

ACKNOWLEDGMENTS

First, we would like to thank our Father God, our Lord and Savior, Jesus Christ, for without Him, we would be nothing, and the Holy Spirit for guiding, keeping, and comforting us.

We would like to thank Chan and Mya who have persevered and prayed alongside of us through the many trials, as well as rejoicing during the good times. We love you!

We would like to thank the many supporters who believed God with us even when they may not have understood.

Donna Brown, we thank you for allowing God to use you prophetically by confirming this book and many more to come. We love you!

Lucy Wise, "Momma Lucy," thank you for your endless, selfless financial support. We thank you because you never questioned why but always displayed compassion in our many times of need! For that, we are forever grateful. Love you!

To the memory of the late Pastor Randy D. Hall, who spoke prophetically into our lives and gave us hope, clarity, and understanding during our most difficult times; may he rest in peace.

To our close friends, who have been there during the difficult seasons: Tim and Angel Rollins, Valerie Somerville, Feji and Tammy McKay, James and Chiquilla Scott, Val Poe, Rev. Charles Murdaugh and the church family; we love you all dearly!

To Pastor David Stanley, Pastor Jonathan Mitchell, Pastor Leonard Wilson, Pastor Kenneth Johnson, Pastor John Wilson and Bishop Styland Scott: you kept me preaching when no one else would call on me because "preachers need to preach…." Thanks a million!

Many thanks to our parents, family, and friends. God bless you all!

– Kevin and Stephanie Lipsey

TABLE OF CONTENTS

Dedication
Acknowledgments
Preface

Introduction	13
Chapter 1: Kevin's Story	19
Chapter 2: Stephanie's Story	37
Chapter 3: The Meeting—28 Days	53
Chapter 4: Two Becoming One—The Truth	65
Chapter 5: Cast Out, but Not Destroyed—Satan's Plot	91
Chapter 6: God's Boot Camp	125
Chapter 7: We Found Rest	151
Chapter 8: The Wilderness—The Sum of All Things	169

POEMS BY KEVIN L. LIPSEY, SR.

The Iniquity	17
The Woman I Knew Not	56
What Good is Good?	78
Why Me?	89
I Had to Be the One	141
These Four Walls	150

PREFACE

You are in for the ride of your life! This is a true story of a couple and their mission in knowing God through "waiting." We are familiar with the Scripture, "those who wait upon the Lord shall renew their strength..." and yes, Scripture is true! However, what is not explained in that passage is how. What my husband and I have learned while waiting is that God will allow a series of trials and wilderness seasons, which, in retrospect, can last as long as the Master desires. During this time, God shapes and molds by teaching us how to trust Him while building our faith with our backs against the wall. When the wilderness season is ordained by God, He uses it to bring order, balance, and harmony in our life.

This book emerges out of two people—my husband and me—attending several churches over a span of years, experiencing activities in life opposite of what we were hearing. This disparity caused us to dig deeper into the Word, seeking God to give understanding, and to reveal His plan for our family. After growing and learning through the "waiting," we discovered our testimonies and life stories weren't weird at all; but in contrast, were ordained by God that we may help others.

It is our prayer that the transparency displayed in this book will help you discover the power in waiting because once the Father finishes, you will possess renewed strength. You'll walk in completeness and be filled with His love, wisdom and understanding. The love of Christ is made strong through our weaknesses, and His love will carry you through the wilderness seasons, which are sure to occur on this journey called Life.

– Stephanie S. Lipsey

Introduction

Forget what you've been told and even more so what you think you know! Haven't we all heard that statement at one time or another? My wife and I thought we had come to know God, especially after being mentored and tutored and engaging in many intense studies; however, all of these studies and disciplines could not prepare us for the trials and lessons we would learn under the tutelage of God Himself. That built-up-on foundation previously sought gave us a false sense of security and answering that one inevitable question: "What is waiting on God?" proved impossible.

Today, we have been given "twelve-step" strategies that promise to somehow propel us into instant gratification, rather than searching out God. Seeking God produces growth in our getting to know Him. We are subject to Him, and in our understanding that His ways are not ours, we learn He does things rather different—simply because He's sovereign.

Over the years we have been told a great deal of supposed facts. We have quantifiably seen more of what we thought we knew, which was, in essence, questionable. In my understanding, many of these so-called facts we have learned have produced incorrect doctrinal issues that many believers embrace today. Many of them have caused God's people to err; spawning un-calculative events in the lives of those who are in the pursuit of finding God.

In my examination of this fallen litmus, I am convinced that the essential fundamentals of the Word of God, which are infallible, should cause us to impose some self-examination. Simply put, too many believers have abandoned the Word and replaced it with "their own understanding."

While we've been trying to achieve wealth and riches from an enormous amount of deceit, we fail to grow and mature in the matters of God, thereby never coming into the knowledge of the truth.

For years my wife and I have tried to fit in the methodology of church as it is today, and we have discovered that waiting on God, however difficult, always works out for our good. Many have fallen from God due to the flaws of man's doctrine, and some have fallen away from God because of the man.

Many of these wolves in sheep's clothing have promised a life filled with immense pleasure, but never a life exemplifying godly character, sacrifice, love, hardship, pain, and waiting on God. We have seen a side of God that would humiliate one's self-image and call in to question why we would follow such a God. The debilitating circumstances in which we found ourselves in and of itself is as much as necessary to our spiritual growth as water to the body; however, today's teaching would suggest otherwise.

To be perfectly clear, my wife and I do believe in blessings, but we also believe blessings come with maturity and development through inevitable hardships and afflictions that produce godly character. Knowing God through the fellowship of His suffering can only come when you wait on Him. Psalm 37:34, "Wait for the LORD and keep His way, and He will exalt you to inherit the land...." [Holman Christian Standard Bible]

"Many are the afflictions of the righteous..." (Psalm 34:19; ESV), but God delivers us out of them all because God wants to grow us through the waiting. My wife and I had to learn this process the hard way.

Chapter 1: Kevin's Story

This book contains our story of two people who discovered the importance of waiting on God. Our Heavenly Father broke down everything we thought we knew about Him and the way He does things! We would discover His love through hardship and pain, while celebrating Him in times of joy!

This is a story of how God delivered us out of the afflictions He allowed us to experience. Through stories, poems, quotes and ministering moments, we will take you on our journey, which was filled with twist and turns, ups and downs. You may want to cry or laugh or even question yourself or your own faith. Please join my wife and me in our times of happiness and sadness as God moved us toward maturity and His purpose for our lives. These pages contain our story—our testament to the glory of God.

WAITING ON GOD

The Iniquity

It came down through my bloodline
Until it reached me—oh, the stain and the pain
The misfortune of my iniquity.
I didn't ask, but yet
I inherited such anguish.
It will rule my life
Because of my ignorance.
Over this period of time, have I thought to choose
Against the iniquity that without Christ I lose?
I've always had an ear by which to hear,
But how can I when my faith has preserved fear?
How can I escape these walls
That entrap me from being free
Of all the pain, the anguish of my iniquity?
Coping with myself daily,
I soon start to get discouraged.
Someone, help me to Christ—
Will He ever come?

WAITING ON GOD

Chapter 1: Kevin's Story

Before time became a reality, allowing us to see what is before today, I stood before an Almighty God. I was whole. This meeting took place in heavenly quarters before the foundations of the earth when God began to construct His plan. The preparations would be simple for the Almighty, Who stands alone as the sole Creator of heaven and earth, but I would have to withstand the test of time.

I was fully equipped in this meeting; to me had been given everything I needed to endure. As I said, I was whole. Once I reached my earthly starting point, a part of me would be separated from me. I would have to search for this part for it would be the missing component I would need to accomplish my assignment. I would have to re-learn of the Almighty God, receive instruction from Him, carry out my task, conquer in His name, and return victorious to Him. In my search, I would even encounter hardship and pain, difficulties, trials and tribulations.

For my time and purpose had been set, I had acknowledged my orders, and my family had been chosen. The time had come for me to be born.

The Beginning

I was born in a time where my mother was thought to be a beautiful young lady, or so I'm told. The daughter of a preaching deacon and an evangelist, my mother had strong family principles. I am fairly sure that's why she was so spectacular to many, but she only allowed my biological father to bedazzle her. I am also told he was quite the catch himself, and not long after they met in the year of 1972, I was born on August 28. Sure, I know I was the cutest infant a person could have ever seen! I was complete with fat cheeks and pretty soft hair with brown mocha skin—at least I would like to think so! Not a lot can be said about the city in which I was born, except it is a city by the ocean, dressed with beautiful palm trees and great seafood. If you happen to be retiring, it's the place to be!

My mother and my father never married, so my father wasn't an important part of my life. My life wasn't anything like my mother had envisioned, and neither did I, for that matter.

It's curious how the beginning of a person's life shapes the rest of his life and how patterns characterize that person's living; nevertheless, destiny had been set and was now in motion. My mother was a great mother, who led a strict household and took us to church. She reared us in the things of God and basically did everything she had been taught by her mother. My grandparents were God-fearing people, so my mother had great teachers.

I wasn't the only child at that time. I was already someone's little brother, and in those days, an unmarried woman with two children did not look good on a résumé. Remember how I mentioned patterns shaping one's life? Well, it was beginning, and my mother could not have known; but we will get to that later.

My mother finally married, and it seemed like the right choice! Or was it? She married a preacher, which catapulted our status in the church. We became preacher's kids. Looking back, this status change was strategically designed by God—not by my mother. My life was unknowingly being shaped by God, but led by my mother, and now my stepfather and I couldn't do any-

Chapter 1: Kevin's Story

thing about it.

My childhood was about as normal as any child could have. My days consisted of attending school, playing with family members, and who can forget, "Church!"

The fact that I was seemingly in church every day of the week didn't appear normal to me. I soon discovered that we were not ordinary (normal), but again, we had status. In addition, I did have lots of family members and plenty of friends; we saw each other quite often. As you can imagine, because we all attended the same church, they too shared my abnormal discrepancy. Things were fun in those days. I mean, my favorite cousin and I were tyrants. We would run around the church, along with our crew and give the ushers a reason to want to get paid. We would chew gum and throw spitballs at grownups, talk back, and always find a reason to go to the bathroom, all while hitting people up for money every chance we got. Needless to say, we saw a great deal of spankings, but we still managed to get the money!

We were happy, of course, to have a father, and I'm sure my mother was as equally happy to have a husband (a promising one). He was good for us. We were a great family, but he came with a price.

Let me pause right here to say: "The end of a thing is better than its beginning and the patient in spirit is better than the proud..." (Ecclesiastes 7:8). My life had begun, and I was now on a course to learn this very lesson. Foundations—be it good or bad—are crucial to a person's life. I would have to learn the importance of waiting on God, and for this reason, I must help you understand this essential truth.

What is "waiting on God?" What does waiting involve? What does it mean to wait?

Waiting on God is simply "God maturing us spiritually"—ultimately causing us to be joined together to meet the complete purpose that God has for our life. The Hebrew rendering of waiting means "to lie in wait for someone; to expect, await, look for patiently, hope; to be confident and to be enduring." All of these qualities are what caps us to the finished work of Christ—that we may be transformed into His image.

My life started with a purpose and decision. The purpose was God's, and the decision involved the people who brought me into the world. Whether or not their decision was to seek God's purpose in order to bring God's intention to pass (somewhat the easy way) or if they were making decisions based on what they thought was best, they unknowingly chose the hard way.

As you will see, my parents did teach us. As I have stated, the Word of God and the definition of "waiting on God" was indeed implemented; notwithstanding, my biological father was not present. Therefore, the result had already determined my outcome; I would have to go the hard way.

For this reason, we have what I call "the what-if clause." No matter what goes on in our life and the decisions made concerning it, God always has a way to bring us ultimately into His will.

"The What-If Clause"

"And we know that all things work together for good to them that love God, to them who are the called according to his purpose. For whom he did foreknow, he also did predestinate to be conformed to the image of his Son, that he might be the firstborn among many brethren. Moreover whom he did predestinate, them he also called: and whom he called, them he also justified: and whom he justified, them he also glorified" (Romans 8:28, 29).

Patterns that can often characterize a life found their way within mine. Fortified within my mother, these patterns affected the way my life was now headed. Since my mother never married my biological father, neither she nor my birth father waited on the Lord. Am I saying that I was a mistake? Most certainly not! I was meant to be!

Chapter 1: Kevin's Story

My stepfather was good to us, but he was the product of the clause. I had no clue that my natural father had also been called to the ministry, as I would be later on.

I will address that matter later. Nevertheless, a pattern had emerged with my mother; first, by having me without the benefit of marriage and consequently marrying my stepfather, whom she eventually divorced. Although he had taught me the Word of God and issues concerning life, I was already affected by an evolving pattern. The decision-making that had governed my life as a child suggested that I would be set on a course to be broken by God—for the called intended.

My mother's assessments on her life determined what she taught me; she did not know that not marrying my birth father would drastically change my being, while simultaneously setting her course and mine. Eventually, as I stated, the unavoidable occurred; she divorced. I still got the call, but boy, did it ever come with a price. Now, I want to get back to my life story and how the importance of "waiting on God" all began.

Going Somewhere?

When my older brother, my two younger siblings, and I were old enough, my parents uprooted us from our home in Savannah and moved to Atlanta. I must tell you that I was so frightened. My older brother cried for four straight hours! My mother couldn't get him to stop; even after she threatened to spank him, he kept on crying. I was so angry with him because he was my big brother, and I looked up to him. Here he was crying like a baby because he did not want to leave Savannah. We were going somewhere.

Eventually we arrived, and I must say that the skyline in Atlanta was breathtaking. I had never seen anything like it before in my life! We moved into a small south side neighborhood and quickly got situated. From where we lived, I could still see that beautiful horizon. Bear in mind, I was in a strange place far from my favorite cousin and my family among never-before-seen unfamiliar faces; however, here in Atlanta I would connect with my destiny.

I soon started school and was quickly faced with challenges. Friends were very hard to come by in those days, but somehow my brother adjusted very well. I was forced to entertain myself while my brother thrived, and because of his ability to adjust, he became very popular. Meanwhile, I spiraled into an internal depression, which made me feel insignificant and just plain ugly.

I thought that I was the ugliest person in the world, and that the only reason why people even acknowledged me was because I was my brother's little sibling. I was living in a strange place, and I was finally feeling what my brother felt coming here—alone and confused. This isolation and confusion would later lead me to some terrible years of having self-confidence issues, low self-esteem, feelings of unworthiness and rejection, and ultimately feeling ashamed of who God had made me.

I had so many questions, and even though I had a mother and a stepfather, they went unanswered. However, that lack of attention was probably due to the younger two children, but "everything was beautiful in tinsel town," or so the family thought.

Remember when I told you that my stepfather came with a price? He moved us to Atlanta, and ultimately my purpose was revealed. And yes, he did take us to church, so hang on to your bootstraps because you will see how the decisions we make can determine certain outcomes in life and the importance of waiting on God. Well, here we go.

The Unveiling

By now we had moved, grown a little, and though some things were great, some things weren't. However, nothing you think you know or guess will prepare you for what I am about to share regarding my story. Some serious issues were manifested in our

Chapter 1: Kevin's Story

family; some I knew, but of others, I had no knowledge. These issues involved lies and deception lurking within the walls of family, and they began showing with ours. We children noticed the arguments, but in all marriages, having arguments is normal, right? I mean, after all, we at least had food, we went to great schools, and we had what we needed. Arguing wasn't the problem—at least that's what I thought. We always had clothing and, on holidays, my parents made a great performance, so that wasn't it either. We always attended church because, by now, my stepfather was the pastor of his own ministry. Still, something was seriously wrong.

I remember when we moved from that small house to a home that, in my mind, was the biggest house that I had seen in my life at that time. This house was complete with five bedrooms—three upstairs and two downstairs in the basement. My two brothers, my sister, and I loved that house. We would do everything in that house. We even fashioned a skating rink in the basement where we would skate every chance we had. We also had a music room downstairs where we would listen to my dad's old Gospel 45s. We even had a large backyard complete with a homemade half-basketball court. We were living the dream.

Music was an important part of my life then and still is today. I was a talented kid; I was not only a gifted singer, but I played drums and the piano. I was also a sketch artist, a writer-poet, a gymnast, and a comedian; I could do it all.

Things Hit the Fan

Not long afterward while still living in a dream (however short it seemed), we found ourselves faced with devastating news. We had to move. I couldn't believe it! The dream was over. My mother was very angry because my stepfather had misappropriated funds. Now whether or not that's true, I do not know. However, the outcome determined this very real moment, and the upshot was, we were moving.

I am also told that my grandmother rendered my mother some advice as well as encouragement. A beautiful and loving woman, Grandma didn't mind telling the truth; she was an evangelist. She had previously conveyed to my mother that marrying my stepfather would be filled with adversity, but the decision had been made. Now my mother would have to learn to lick her own wounds.

My stepfather had many hidden issues, many of which plagued his life. To this point, these issues had stayed somewhat concealed. But now, with the house, his wife, and the future of four children, his problems had begun manifesting and affecting our lives.

We began noticing that he would sometimes disappear and tell my mother that he was away on business for his job; however, he would always be back in time for church. My mother had no reason to suspect anything was amiss. Then she started noticing that his work-related absences were becoming a pattern, and soon, she began receiving reports that people had indeed seen him in another part of town.

These reports caused even more problems as you can well imagine because the information not only raised trust issues, but also the nagging question: what is he hiding? The situation grew progressively worse over a period of years, and while my mother confronted him, he continued to build a web of lies.

He began inviting some new friends to church, and sometimes he even invited them to our house. We noticed these male friends were overly effeminate, and we felt something was very wrong with this picture. They were all so overly nice, we suspected they were gay. Of course, this corroborated what other people had claimed and tried to tell my mother, but she didn't listen to them because she simply didn't believe the negative reports.

My stepfather had apparently been spotted on the side of town where the gay crowd hung out. Needless to say, when things finally hit the fan, it was more than bad; it was really bad.

Chapter 1: Kevin's Story

As the second oldest of four children, I didn't feel the effects at the time that my eldest brother did. However, I did not realize how I had internalized the situation until later in my life when it manifested. My other siblings were too young at the time to be affected.

Of course, the backdrop to all of this upset resulted in my stepfather's leaving us one cold winter. He had left prior to this time, but never like this and never for that long. But the truth was out; he was gay! Although he continued to deny it then, he has come to terms in recent years. He has confessed his sin and is currently working on his life. My prayer is that he will be delivered from it and be made free.

A Real Moment

In spite of what is seen and heard, people are told and made to believe in mass media forums that homosexuality is a normal and natural part of life. Some even say that they were "born" that way. While we all are born in sin, this belief, however, is a sick, twisted untruth. We all were born in sin and shaped in iniquity with many different generational issues, but what we are not told is that in the beginning God originally had something to say about this matter.

In fact, the Bible clearly explains that God vehemently discourages such acts and deems them abominable. The only natural sense surrounding this matter is that God told us this abomination would happen and His decisive disapproval of it.

Still, with all of this, very little concern is shown toward the family members who are left to cope with the effects of such acts. I will address this matter in my upcoming book.

We tend to hide behind the art of confession while evading its true meaning. Confession should lead us in realizing that we have strayed away from God's original truth.

"For the wrath of God is revealed from heaven against all

ungodliness and unrighteousness of men, who suppress the truth in unrighteousness" (Romans 1:18; KJV).

This verse is the standard which we should follow.

True confession should not only reveal this exactness, but would also bring forth pure contrition. Being contrite leads to true repentance; a repentant heart agrees with God that we are sinful. We are then granted salvation, and from there we are delivered. The Scripture tells us to "let God be true and every man a liar."

God has declared that man with man, and woman with woman are un-natural, lustful, and a shameful abomination. However, the world shows the opposite. God's standard demands that we exercise our right to choose; His love for us suggests that we should choose Him and His way.

A Ministering Moment

My mother had received overwhelming news. I can imagine how disturbed, hurt, confused, and baffled she was. How shocking was this news—or was it?

My mother began receiving phone calls from men cursing her with anger, calling her awful names, and emphasizing that she was to leave "their man" alone. Remember when I told you that my stepfather came with a price? Well, this hireling finally cashed in.

I 'm told that my grandmother and someone from his side of the family never wanted my mother to marry my stepfather—not because they thought that my mother was better or that he himself was a bad person. Rather, they could see something my mother couldn't. Grandma had been around the block a few times and knew more in-depth matters about the family into which my mother was about to marry. My mother, of course, was a grown woman who was capable of making her own decisions; however, she did not listen to the advice of her mother

Chapter 1: Kevin's Story

and the other person. She missed the importance of "waiting on God."

This decision affected not only her life, but ours too. Patterns that characterize one's life had infected my stepfather, my mother and now us. We are told in the Word of God to "…lean not unto thine own understanding… acknowledge him, and he shall direct thy paths" (Proverbs 3:5, 6).

First Peter 4:12-14 (KJV) reads:

> "Beloved, think it not strange concerning the fiery trial which is to try you, as though some strange thing happened unto you: But rejoice, inasmuch as ye are partakers of Christ's sufferings; that, when his glory shall be revealed, ye may be glad also with exceeding joy. If ye be reproached for the name of Christ, happy are ye; for the spirit of glory and of God rests upon you: on their part he is evil spoken of, but on your part he is glorified."

What does this passage mean, you might ask? The answer may surprise you.

Remember when I told you to forget what you think you know? Well, here goes.

When my mother decided to marry my stepfather, she was told by God through her mother and others not to marry him. My mother decided to do it anyway.

The clause was then activated on the behalf of the called, so because of this, God allowed it. My stepfather was also called, but he didn't deal with his issues. Because the two became one, his issue became the foundation which God would use to bring me (us) to meet the complete purpose that God had for my life. My mother should not have thought these things strange, for she too was called of God, as well as me.

I have already mentioned that my own birth father was also called, and I came out of his loins. He had the call of a pastor on his life, but he never answered. The Bible suggests that God uses a man and his seed. I was his seed, and his call was passed down to me.

To his own birth son (my brother), my stepfather was what my biological father meant to me. In that regard, he had a call that his son would one day assume; but for me, a hireling. Exactly what is a hireling?

A hireling is a person who works only for pay, especially in menial or boring jobs with little or no concern for the value of the work.

My stepfather didn't marry or father us for pay; however, I want to point out something of significance. While he may not have done these things for pay due to the increasing need to fulfill his desires, he inadvertently had little concern for the value of family work and to see it through. By default, no matter how much he claimed he loved us, we became insignificant. My stepfather started off great. Again, he taught us the Word, took us to church and even provided for us, but a true man of God versus a hireling patterns himself after Jesus Christ (the Good Shepherd).

I find it interesting that the word menial means "lowly and sometimes degrading, servile; submissive—humble."

Philippians 2:5-8 says,

> "Let this mind be in you, which was also in Christ Jesus: 6Who, being in the form of God, thought it not robbery to be equal with God: 7But made himself of no reputation, and took upon him the form of a servant, and was made in the likeness of men: 8And being found in fashion as a man, he humbled himself, and became obedient unto death, even the death of the cross."

It takes a man of God of this caliber not only to train up a child, but to teach him from the Word and to even provide and remain until death do them part. To be like Christ and see it through

Chapter 1: Kevin's Story

even unto death is what pleases God. My stepfather didn't fulfill this charge; he obviously had deeper issues than previously known which prohibited him from his total responsibility.

Even though my biological father wasn't there, I still had a man of God in watch care (service) over me, and for that I will be forever grateful. Now my stepfather has to contend with the Lord concerning his calling and whether or not he is pleasing unto God. (There is a more excellent way.)

The more excellent way is ultimately God's way, and although my parents seemingly predetermined their way, we all were inevitably affected by their decision.

The Aftermath

Years had now passed and many issues surfaced, but the one true problem still remained, which was, "the unveiling. " Seeing the demise of a once beautiful family with incredible potential was awful. We were once the example among families in a time where families were not popular; we were a model for the many who followed in our path.

Needless to say, we eventually closed our church, and the sheep scattered. "Woe unto the shepherd who destroys and scatters the sheep." However, not long after a few tries, my mother and stepfather divorced. Their marriage was finally over, but by this time, the damage had been done. My course was now set, and boy, was I damaged.

The Terrible Years (Before the Break-up)

During all of this madness, I went through a period where I became angry. I took my anger and frustration out wherever I could during these terrible years. I spiraled into an internal depression, and now, with this issue, I was led to places that I wasn't prepared to go.

Many problems existed within our household. Let's face it, try blending a family together while keeping secrets, and oh, yeah, living in a city far from what you are used too. So I snapped and began to familiarize myself with the identity of a tyrant. We became a family in shambles—constantly moving and always having very little money. So I turned to the streets for comfort.

So many problems were hidden within the four walls of our family. While I recall many of these unfortunate issues, it's important to mention that my siblings were equally affected. Patterns were emerging in their lives; however, each of us as well as our parents had to find our way in God.

I found myself failing miserably in high school, and honestly, I simply didn't care. My parents were tripping, and our home was just another very unstable place, so I did what was presented to me by my friends. I started stealing cars and getting into trouble. Don't worry, I've paid my debt to society; I'm good.

Yes, I was a car thief. I must admit that I was pretty good at it too. There is a connection here. Do you recall that movie, Gone in Sixty Seconds with Nicholas Cage? Well, that was just a movie because he had nothing on me. Sixty seconds was too long—way too long. For me, it was more like gone in fifteen seconds, and I'm not kidding.

I was stealing so much that I became very good at it. I was even approached by certain people who wanted me to steal car parts for them, but I wouldn't because I was simply having fun. My mother tried to get me to stop, but she represented one of the objects of my hurt. She was talking out of the side of her neck as far as I was concerned; I only wanted to have fun. Well, having that fun landed me in jail several times, and being in jail was no fun at all.

Now I will explain some things. You see, like my parents I had issues generated by them and the choices (or decisions) they had made concerning our family. Paul said in the eleventh chapter of First Corinthians, "Be ye followers of me, even as I also am of Christ" (v. 1; KJV). Even though it wasn't often expressed verbally, I followed some horrible patterns.

The idea of this verse is to be an example of Christ—a

Chapter 1: Kevin's Story

life that people can see and emulate. Although my parents did a great deal of this, I somehow gravitated to the issues at hand (characterizing patterns) and consequently made the wrong decisions—legitimately so, but wrong.

I was at an age where I was making my own decisions, and that meant when I disobeyed my parents or didn't heed their advice (like my mother did with her mother), I would have to suffer every consequence. I know, I know! You're probably thinking "That's not right," but consider this… I was now on my journey with the Lord, and like my mother, I could listen or reject. I chose to reject, and as a result, I would face even more consequences.

The Children Are Here

Not long afterward while still in my rebellious years, I was in and out of the church. I was playing drums for choirs and stealing a car or two to get to rehearsals. In the midst of it all, I met someone. At the time, she was nice—very nice. (Guys know what I mean.) We would meet in school under interesting circumstances that I won't get into, but we hit it off pretty well.

In any case, we began dating and soon engaged in adult acts before marriage (neither of us were abstaining at the time). Afterward came my firstborn child—a girl. Our relationship then became difficult, but she and I stayed in the rocky situation and later a son followed.

Needless to say, we didn't marry. We talked about it, but I was in my tyrant years. I wasn't supposed to be doing the things I was doing—not to mention having kids at a young age, but the children were now here. There was no going back.

Let me take a moment and pause for the cause

A pattern had emerged just like my mother's in times past. Here I was with two children and refusing to marry their mother. We were never supposed to marry; however, we did "married people things," and therefore my children were summoned to this world.

Now, here are two thoughts. First, you may be thinking, "Well, I could say that about my mother." However, ponder this: whether or not my mother and natural father were supposed to be married or my children's mother and I were supposed to be married is not the focus. The real point I am making is that my father's absence was the key; he simply wasn't there. The devil loves to get fathers absent from their children.

My biological father chose to stay away from me, so I didn't benefit from that relationship. Although my mother married another man, that choice eventually backfired on her. The fact that she married that particular person eventually affected us too. Even though I never married my children's mother, I planned to be a part of their lives. If I could help it, I did not want to be absent.

When my children were younger, I was there for them emotionally. I talked with them regularly, taught them about the Word, took them to church as much as I could (they didn't live with me), and cared for them. My father left his child rearing up to someone else. I am not saying that I did not appreciate my stepfather; rather, I am only saying that "my biological father wasn't there!"

Fathers are fundamental to a child's life. It is my belief that society forgets exactly how much. Therefore, we perpetuate the mistakes made by our parents before us. I mentioned that the devil loves to get fathers to be absentee. He also loves to get them angry, aloof, and addicted.

My father could have been there because my mother didn't keep him from me; however, he chose to opt out. The pattern he left for me was impregnating someone and not rearing the children (not by my choice), but I was determined not to let that happen—even though I was already in knee-deep.

My second thought: Children are never a mistake! We

Chapter 1: Kevin's Story

must understand that, in these situations, we, the parents, are the ones who are being disobedient. The consequence of my being intimate before marriage caused my having to rear children before I was properly prepared for them.

It's not the fact that I wasn't supposed to have children, but I was to have them at the right moment in time. My children came out of me, and they are my seed. I simply planted the seed at the wrong time. Remember, the intimate marital relationship was created for marriage because God ordained it to be so. This means that the sex act, which was created for marriage to procreate did what it was purposed to do; however, I was the one who advanced it with haste. Because I failed to follow God's divine order—dating, marriage, sex, children—I had to face some consequences.

> "Inevitably, what God said and establishes will come to pass in life; good or bad, it's coming to pass…" – Kevin L. Lipsey, Sr.

So here I am with two children, living at home with my parents, and the home front is in trouble. Because my parents were seemingly miserable, almost nothing would cause them to get agitated at us. Like clockwork, they would put my brothers and me out of the house onto the streets—at times for no apparent reason. I hated these times, which happened quite often. The home front became so bad that they would leave to go out of town, lock us out the house, and wave goodbye! "What is that, America?!!"

Eventually, I moved on and grew up. After giving my life to Christ, I started to rely on the Lord rather than my botched relationship with my parents. It was time to go on to new things, and I was ready. I began participating more in area churches after leaving my stepfather's ministry.

Subsequently, I was later called into the ministry to preach the gospel, though I didn't start to preach until years later. Whoa! After I had two children and all that I had done, I now have this call? In my mind it didn't add up! However, I would later answer the call, and my life would change forever.

Let me also say that just because I answered "the call" on my life did not mean I didn't have to suffer the consequences of my poor decision-making. In fact, my children's mother would later become my nemesis because of our juvenile behavior of having children prematurely. This reality not only ignited my interest and caused me to take ministry very seriously, but set me on a pattern of epic proportions with my children's mother that ultimately caused problems with my offspring.

Over the following years after being in ministry, I married my first wife. We did not stay married for long because our relationship never should have happened. We were manipulated into marrying; and shortly afterward, we parted ways.

This is what led me to my destiny, and I was now on track to receive my greatest blessing of all—my true wife sent from God!

Chapter 2: Stephanie's Story

Nevils, Georgia. Haven't heard of the place, huh? Don't worry, many have not. Well, Nevils is located about thirty miles from Statesboro, Georgia—about forty- five miles from Savannah. This small country town shaped many of the values that I hold close today. When traveling to Statesboro, you would take I-16, which is a long highway filled with trees, open fields, crops and livestock. I-16 doesn't offer much in the way of scenery, yet the way can be enlightening during certain seasons. Once you exit the highway toward Cochran, you are sure to run into dirt roads, chicken houses, cotton and tobacco fields, as you travel toward your destination: Nevils, Georgia.

My mother and two of her brothers were reared by their grandparents in Nevils, Georgia. While living in a time period of the impending racial prejudices among whites and people of color in the South, my mother endured a rough childhood. She has told me stories of her first year of attending a high school that was in its first year of desegregation. The whites did not want the blacks attending "their" school and vice-versa. Already at odds with the whites, she then had to face the issue of color among blacks. Due to the fact that my mom was very fair-skinned, she was picked on by the darker-skinned people of color. They would tease her and call her "white-girl." These times presented difficult challenges for my mother. Her greatest times were when she would get out of the house, visit her cousins, attend football games, sing in the choir, and participate in other church activities. As a teenager, after she would help her grandfather, who was a sharecropper, finish with the crops, she started to spend summers in Macon, Georgia, with her mother, where eventually she would meet my dad.

My mother birthed me at a young age, and in an era where it was shameful to get pregnant without being married. During those times, family values were very important as well as the integrity thereof. Moral standards were at an all-time high—not that the sins weren't being committed; they were simply hidden.

As a result, my mother, out of fear, concealed her pregnancy from her grandparents and even my father. She had been dating a guy in Nevils, and when the pregnancy was exposed, everyone assumed he was the father; however, both he and my mother knew differently. Due to decisions made prior my birth, the patterns set in motion were starting to take form...

My Beginning

I was born on June 1, 1973, in Statesboro, Georgia, and since my biological father had no knowledge of me, my mother's grandfather stepped in as "Daddy." My great-grandfather, who was a share cropper, was a businessman with employees in the early 70s until he retired.

By the time I was one, he had saved enough money to buy almost an acre of land—0.99 of an acre to be exact. He built his own brick home with three bedrooms, one and a half bathrooms, and an attached carport—all for the sum of about $27,000 cash. This was quite an accomplishment for a black man during those days. He also was a deacon in the church he attended, and he lived his life as a Godly man with veracity. He was a great man

Chapter 2: Stephanie's Story

who helped to rear me as his own, and he was very instrumental in the development of my childhood and who I would become.

While my great-grandfather was making a living for the family, my great-grandmother made sure the house was held together. She was a strong woman of God, who had overcome many issues in her own life, and God blessed her to be a good helpmate for her husband. She was a great cook and later worked long hours at the school in that town. She lived to be well in her seventies.

I had a great time in the "country" as we would call it, and since I was the first niece, grand, and great-granddaughter, I pretty much got everything I wanted, to say the least. However, the evil spirits that still lingered were on a mission to abort God's plan for my life, and little did I know that some stormy nights were ahead.

Our Launch to Macon

When I was two years old, my mother moved us to Macon, Georgia, where her mother, two brothers, and a sister lived. She began to start her new journey of life "in the city" in order to make a better life for us. After my mom moved to Macon, she would see my biological father around town, and they even started to date again. Still, she never told him about me. He would even suggest that I was his child, but to no avail; she would not confirm his suspicions.

Due to the fear and rejection that had occurred earlier in her life, which had kept her in bonds and chains, my mother kept me a secret. A few years passed, and my mom met and started to date another man whom she ultimately married. He was much older and had a nice way about himself.

My mother's new husband was a good provider and a disciplinarian, but he had a problem with alcohol and extreme jealousy. It wasn't long before he started to physically and verbally abuse my mother, which started my beginning to long for my biological father.

My First Spiritual Encounter

As a young girl my mother would send me to the "country" in Nevils, which I absolutely loved. My great-grandparents provided stability and a sense of peace—a peace that was missing at home due to the many fights between my mother and stepdad.

At the time, I was the only grandchild, so I was showered with much love and joy. God used my summers in the country as a way of escape for me. These became my times of safety and security, which I lacked at home. During those days I could play with my cousins, spend time with my uncle James, go skating, and simply enjoy being a kid; however, the nightmares never subsided.

My grandparents were unaware of the issues my mom was experiencing because I had been instructed to keep silent on these matters. The fear my mother's situation presented was constant, but somehow I learned to pray at an early age for the safety of my mother. The heartache at home was so troublesome to me that one night I had a nightmare about the fighting and woke up screaming and shouting, "Please don't kill my mom!" My grandparents questioned me about my dream, and I finally spilled the whole shebang. I needed an outlet, and my grandparents listened. I was relieved that someone else was now informed of my tainted family.

Unknowingly, a different aspect of the fear that my mother had possessed as a teenager had now been passed on to me—on a greater level. I spent many years fearful that my mom was going to expire at the hands of my stepfather. At an early age when children should feel safe, I begin to pray to God for protection while huddled in the corners of our home as they would fight, hoping that God would eventually prevail. The fear was so severe that a spiritual door was opened in my life. God was drawing me closer to Him, but the demonic world was starting

Chapter 2: Stephanie's Story

to take notice.

One night as a seven- or eight-year-old, while visiting my great-grandparents for the summer, I prepared for bed with my great-grandmother. (During those days, she and her husband slept in different rooms.) I was awakened by her screaming and yelling, and I saw a black, animal-looking creature pulling her leg, trying to get her out of bed. I started screaming and pulling her in the opposite direction toward me. My great-grandfather came running into the bedroom, turned on the light, and yelled "What's ailing y'all?!!"

We were both crying and trying to explain what was happening; however, the creature we had both seen was now gone. Until the day that my great-grandmother passed, we would recount the story, explaining that we were both in the same bad dream. Not until my adult life did I understand that what had happened was not a dream, but a real demonic encounter.

The door of fear had been opened, and the evil spirits walked right in. My eyes were now opened to the spirit world and, as a result, I would never be the same. As a teenager, I would have visitations and see tall, dark figures in groups of three, towering over my bed. Out of fear, I would jump out of bed screaming, waking everyone in the house. The spiritual attacks continued well into my adult life as evil spirits would taunt me. I would often feel the presence of evil; my heart would start to race while I was sleeping. I would jump out of bed screaming. The best way I could explain these visitations was that I would feel like I was fighting for my life, and if the evil presence caught me, I would die.

My Teenage Years

As I grew older, I started to embellish the joys of life. Things did not seem as drastic as they did in the past, but nonetheless, there were hidden patterns. My parents continued to argue, sometimes fighting intensely, but I had to find a way to maintain some kind of life, right? After a brief separation, my stepfather left and bought a house for the family on the south side of Macon.

I began making friends in this neighborhood, started attending a new school and began to explore the side of town where we now lived. We made this move at the beginning of my first year of middle school, so I was nervous yet very excited. Things was starting to look up for us.

Somehow in the midst of all the quiet chaos, my mother became pregnant and soon after, we welcomed a little brother into the family. The birth of my brother brought some joy and even eased some of the tension between my mom and stepfather. We began to function as a normal family—but only for a little while. My little brother was full of energy, and we never had a dull moment when he was around. I will never forget when he was about four or five; my mother bought him a pair of cowboy boots and did he ever love those boots. If he could have, he would have slept in those boots! No matter what he was wearing, the boots had to accompany his outfit. During winter, spring, summer, and fall, the boots were his choice of shoes to wear.

As my brother got older, the family dynamics became even more strenuous. I was twelve years older, and he was constantly fighting for my attention as well as the attention of others. It would not be until later that I discovered how he often felt left out. Because of my being a teenager, I didn't want to be caught carrying around my little brother. After all, I had other things on my mind at that time.

As I reflect back, my mother was and is a beautiful woman with a kind and gentle spirit. In those days she was small with a petite shape, light-skinned with freckles and long flowing hair. She was hard-working, but she always seemed to be able to make time for my brother and me, allowing us to enjoy the finer things of life. I remember days of going to the park to play, shopping, and oh, I can't forget, visiting the county fair that would come to town every year in October.

Chapter 2: Stephanie's Story

My mother also did a great job of making sure I was grounded in the things of God. She readily involved me in church activities, which became a big part of my life. As a youth, I too, sang in the choir, served as a junior usher, and was on the Sunday school committee. We were members of a Baptist church, which soon would become a place of refuge for my mom and me.

Later, I would discover that church attendance alone wouldn't be enough for the trials I would endure; I need a relationship with the Lord Jesus Christ to see me through. I would need Him because my stepfather's drinking was getting worse, and due to the continuous fighting and arguing in our home, the nightmares and visitations ensued.

Often, I would lash out and declare, "I wish I knew my real father, so I wouldn't have to live here!" These outbursts led to having conversations about our situation with my mom. I would plead with her to leave or if she didn't want to go, to let me go to my grandmother's house. I started to ask my mother questions about my biological father. I wanted to know why he did not try to find me or why he never called or visited. His absenteeism made me feel like I wasn't loved, and a strong sense of fear and rejection would come over me. Like the patterns previously shown with my mother, they were now manifesting in my life.

Seeing me cry and watching my anguish, my mom thought I was old enough to know the truth. At twelve years old, she told me that the person I thought was my father was not the man, and she proceeded to tell me the identity of my biological father. This confession led me in a relentless pursuit to find him. I felt that somehow if he knew what I was going through, he could possibly rescue me.

The Search Begins

One of my birth father's aunts still lived in Macon, so my mom thought that would be a good place to start in our search. So we went to the aunt, and my mom related to her the entire story.

She listened but didn't make any promises, and from time to time we would try to get more information, but to no avail. The aunt did not budge, and she became very resolute in her decision not to help us. She wouldn't give my mom any information—nothing—no numbers and no addresses. She was determined not to mention me to my dad. This went on for about five years. My mother did find out that my father was now married and living in Washington, D.C.

I was very angry at my aunt for a long time; however, looking back as an adult, I believe I can say that I understand. I guess we had placed her in a difficult situation. And she didn't want to be the one responsible for maybe, bringing stress on a seemingly "happy marriage"—even if it was at my expense of growing up without my father.

I do believe that it is important that I take a moment and pause here and offer that, as Christians, it is vitally important to take the time and consult God on every experience that comes our way. No matter how sincere you think your actions may be, your course of action may lead you to think you're making the right decision. However, the writer, Ron Rhodes, made a profound statement in his book entitled The Complete Book of Bible Answers: "One can do things with all sincerity unknowingly that he or she is sincerely wrong."

Sincerely believing something doesn't guarantee its truth. This too is an example of waiting on God. We must pray and wait on the answer from God before making any decision that could ultimately turn the course of another's life. Over the next five years, I continued to think about my father, but the pursuit wasn't as persistent, since my mom was now divorcing my stepfather.

All of the chaos at home had finally come to an end, and we were on our way to healing. I started to take an interest in guys, and when I was old enough to date, I got involved heavily with a young man. Even though I was young, the void I was

Chapter 2: Stephanie's Story

trying to fill was temporarily replaced through relationships. My mom worked on a factory job, which meant I was home alone watching my little brother—just the two of us.

They used to say in the old days, "an idle mind is a devil's workshop" and boy, was he busy. A teenager at home alone without supervision and raging hormones leads to premarital sex—something I am not proud of, nevertheless, I am sharing the truth. Consequently, like my mom, I ended up having a child at a young age.

After graduating from high school, I was accepted into Tuskegee University Engineering Program, and my plans were to become a mechanical engineer. While having the required physical to enter college, I discovered I was pregnant. The whole scenario was very disappointing to my family and me, but my family joined in to help. They embraced my decision to keep the baby.

Add-ons and Take-aways

I think it is important to uncover an unidentified pattern. I have already shared how my mother was not taught about her body, and since the needed talks about intimacy were prohibited in her home, my mom made sure she did not do the same with me. She had taught me the principles of becoming a young lady; I too knew right from wrong and had a sense of consciousness.

My mother stressed the importance of waiting and abstinence; however, after conversations with my aunt, she added her the clause: "I don't want to put you on the pill, but if you think you can't hold out, come and tell me. I will put you on the pill so you will not get pregnant." Because my mother added a clause, she took away the potency of God's Word that was able to keep me in all His ways.

Again, the only foolproof way is God's way. The word tells us in Proverbs 22:6, "Train up a child in the way he should go: and when he is old, he will not depart from it." One of our jobs as parents is to rear our kids according to what God says in His Word—not according to how the world advises us to rear our children. This is the more excellent way God would have us to appropriate. When we make decisions based on our experiences, feelings, or emotions, we tend to fulfill the lust of the flesh rather than allowing the Spirit of God to lead. Consequently, mistakes are made, and patterns are established until they are corrected through God's Word.

A Ministering Moment

Speaking from a woman's perspective, I spend a great amount of time preparing my daughter for her future. Not only do I teach her organizational skills, the importance of personal hygiene and grooming, and lessons pertaining to her growing into a young lady, I spend even more time teaching her godly values and her role as a young lady. When we teach our daughters to reverence God as well as their bodies, they learn to appreciate what they have.

My mother did not learn these lessons from her grandmother. She grew up in a time when the pervading philosophy was "the less you know, the better." However, the Word teaches the opposite in the book of Titus, which says:

> "The aged women likewise, that they be in behavior as becometh holiness, not false accusers, not given to much wine, teachers of good things; That they may teach the young women to be sober, to love their husbands, to love their children, To be discreet, chaste, keepers at home, good, obedient to their own husbands, that the word of God be not blasphemed (2:3-5; KJV).

If we take the advice from the Word of God, as mothers, we would have less of the embarrassing elements that come from not waiting on God.

Chapter 2: Stephanie's Story

The Meeting

Proverbs 3:5-6 admonishes us: "Trust in the Lord with all thine heart; and lean not unto thine own understanding. In all thy ways acknowledge him, and he shall direct thy paths."

One evening when my mother and I were at the Taste of Macon, we ran into my birth father's best friend. Upon laying eyes on me, he uttered, "You look just like Richard!" My mother then explained to him our story and how we were trying to find him. She asked if he could call and give Richard our contact information. He said he would, and we exchanged numbers. I was so excited.

At this time I was about seven or eight months into my pregnancy. It's funny how things happen. Even though God doesn't make mistakes, I made the mistake of not waiting on God. Am I saying my child was a mistake? Of course not; however, God had to inject His clause:

"And we know that all things work together for good to them that love God, to them who are the called according to His purpose" (Romans 8:28).

About a week later, I received a phone call, and it was my father. He told me about the account his friend gave him and wanted to speak to my mom. After they spoke, he got back on the phone with me and asked many questions. One of the first was "What color are your eyes?" (His are a light-brown/greenish color—hazel.) And several additional questions.

He mentioned coming to Macon, and he talked about having a blood test done. I had so much anticipation of meeting him that I was willing to do whatever he asked.

Over the next month, my dad and I talked every single day for hours at a time. It was like a courtship; we wanted to know every single detail about each other, and I couldn't wait to talk to him in person. I was so happy that I had finally found my father. Through many conversations with my dad, I found out that I now had two younger brothers. One was the age of my brother on my mom's side, and the other one was a year and a week older than my son. I also discovered that my father had been adopted at birth, and he had found out about his biological mother at the age of twelve. On top of that, his mom had also been adopted, and she did not find her biological family until 2004. Once again, I saw the evolving of patterns and circumstances; when decisions are made, patterns are established that dictate the course of our lives. Waiting on God is so essential to finding the will of God and positioning ourselves for our destiny in God.

When my dad finally came to visit me in Macon, I had much anticipation and couldn't wait to see him. Upon seeing me, his spirit instantly resonated that I was his daughter. He said he no longer needed the blood test, and the rest is history. (Come to find out, we are both the "O" blood type.) Shortly after our meeting, my child was born on February 14. One chapter was now closed as another was opening.

From a Teen to an Adult

After the birth of my son, I didn't go to Tuskegee as planned; I turned my attention to the art of styling and caring for hair. I decided to get training in the area of cosmetology. This choice seemed like the right fit since I had enjoyed styling hair from the age of five. Once I had a license, my plan was to open my own hair salon. Upon graduating from beauty school, I decided to make a move to Atlanta. I had an uncle who lived there, and I thought this city would be a good place for me. In Atlanta was where I met my first husband. He was a salon owner and a computer technician by trade. He had been married before with three kids (his previous wife was deceased), and he was thirteen years older than me.

Chapter 2: Stephanie's Story

I was very intrigued with his intelligence and charming ways. He was a good provider and a caring man; however, he was a very jealous man—like mother, like daughter. We were only married for three years due to his unresolved issues in his life and those in mine. If only I had the knowledge then of the importance of waiting on God for a spouse that I have now, I believe things may have turned out differently. Our brief marriage was definitely a learning experience, though many of the decisions I made were some of the same ones my mother made. Cycles, patterns, and issues of life can definitely impact a person's life in ways that are perpetually ongoing, that is, until we reach a point of being enlightened.

Waiting on God and learning from Him is vitally necessary to avoid the pitfalls that are in this journey we call life. Jesus says, "He is the way, the truth, and the life." He is the source of our success. I am amazed that even in my faults, impatience, and self-serving ways that His mercy and faithfulness is ever enduring. He is always waiting to lead us into the path of righteousness. Although the marriage ended and we went our separate ways, during that marriage, my next child—a beautiful baby girl—was born.

Like my mother, I married at a young age—one of the patterns that can characterize a person's life. Not really having much experience in the area of dating, after my divorce I went through a time period of doing many things I thought I had missed out on…

The Lord was still pulling on me, but since I was so young and independent, I did not fully surrender to his call. I was too busy dating, getting involved sexually with men (soul-ties), partying, and living the single life. The cycle in my mother's life was starting all over again in mine. I was trying to fill a void that could only be filled by God. I was traveling down a road that was heading for destruction; I needed God to rescue me and to fill my God-void.

The salon in which I worked was Christian-owned and operated. The owner was a beautiful woman of God, and though I had no idea at the time, God had sent me there for a reason. My employer would talk to me about the Lord and subtly minister to me. She had a gentle spirit, and I looked up to her. During the times when my flesh ruled, I felt like she could see my filthiness, so I would try to conceal it. Again, I knew God was calling me higher, and I was finding it increasingly difficult to run away from Him.

I had worked there for about six months when she married and suddenly announced she was moving. Unknown to me, God had instructed her to give me the salon. I was in total shock, crying, and telling her I didn't want the business. I offered all kinds of excuses for not accepting her gift: I had recently divorced, I was rebuilding my clientele, I was a single-parent, and I couldn't afford to run a business. As she kept encouraging me, I finally asked, "How can I afford to run a business?"

"God wants you to step out on faith, and He will take care of you." Fearfully, I accepted her gift, renamed the salon, and became a doubtful salon owner. Little did I know that I was on my way to learning how to trust my Father and to live by faith. This was the start of a new day in my life, and God was just beginning…

God would send people my way to try and lead me to the right path. He would propel people to come to the salon, and they would prophesy over my life. They would speak the word of the Lord concerning my future as God saw me—not as I was at that time. He sent Christian women to work for me, and He managed to surround me with His presence.

It wasn't long before I started growing in the Word of God and becoming greatly convicted when I would surrender to my flesh and not follow the Spirit by restraining myself. Again and again I would make promises to my Father and break them every time. This disappointment in myself led me to make a

Chapter 2: Stephanie's Story

commitment to the Lord.

On a Friday night in my kitchen while singing and praising God, I told the Lord that I wasn't going to date anymore. I didn't want to be involved with another man until He sent me to my husband. I was tired of meeting men who said they were Christians yet tried their best to get me to compromise. I was ready to serve God fully and giving up my temple was no longer an option.

When I prayed that prayer and meant it from my heart, little did I know that my husband was right around the corner...

A Ministering Moment

I would like to stop at this point in my testimony to address waiting on God for your spouse. Many sermons have been preached and many books and songs have been written about this area of life. Praying and seeking God for a mate is the obvious, but what is seldom mentioned is, "the waiting while in preparation."

The story of Esther tells how she spent a year of preparation before she was appointed to be King Ahasuerus's queen.

> Esther 2:12 (KJV): "Now when every maid's turn was come to go in to king Ahasuerus, after that she had been twelve months, according to the manner of the women, (for so were the days of their purifications accomplished, to wit, six months with oil of myrrh, and six months with sweet odours, and with other things for the purifying of the women)."

Not only should this be a time of purification for the outward, but also for the inward. Are you in a position of humility and submission to God in preparation to be submissive to your husband? Do you have a spirit of servanthood? Are you willing to die to your flesh and serve your husband and kids?

Even Jesus came not to be served, but that He might serve

and give Himself to be a ransom for many. Are you ready to give of yourself? Of your service, prayer life, and duty as a wife and mother? These are the questions to be pondered while "waiting on God for a mate."

Once we give ourselves to God and prepare for a mate while patiently waiting, we will not be so quick to make decisions that are not conducive to the will of God. Certain circumstances characterize a person's life and begin to set patterns in motion. My journey positioned itself due to the decisions that were made, which subsequently, would lead to the fulfilling of God's purpose for my life. "And we know that all things work together for the good of them who are the called…" Oh, how important it is to wait on God for instructions on this journey we call life.

Chapter 3:
The Meeting—28 Days

WHAT'S HAPPENING, FOLKS? DO YOU WANT TO HEAR AN unbelievable story? Would you like to hear how a man's life could change in 28 days? Well, it all began awkwardly—some years ago in September of 2000. My family came in town from Savannah, and since my uncle had never skated before that time in his boring life, we decided to go to the skating rink.

As I was getting dressed to go skating, I heard the Holy Spirit say to me, "You are going to meet someone tonight."

I looked up at the ceiling and said, "Yeah, right..." as I continued getting dressed.

At this telling of the story, it is important to know that I was seven months divorced and had been through quite an adventure before what I am about to share in this chapter. You see, I had been praying to the Lord that I might find my "good thing" according to Scripture, but what I stumbled across in the process was, well, it was crazy, which is the only way I know how to describe what happened.

I must go back to the previous year. I recall an attractive young lady whom I had met years before. I'll admit, I was taken. We met again under remarkable circumstances.

I can say that because when I had met her before, we only

saw each other for a moment, and then lost contact. So here she was again in my life—and not for the reason you may be thinking. She was there to prophesy my wife to me, which she did, and I was furious! After all, I had been trying to get with her, and she was telling me about a woman I never knew existed. Oh, my soul.

She would describe my future wife to me, sighting how God had prepared this "mystery woman" exactly for me. Instead of listening, I was saying, "Girl, I'm trying to get with you. You are her!" I did not want to hear about whom she was talking. I responded, "You are talking about some woman who doesn't exist." After trying and failing to date her for quite some time, I stopped annoying her with my advances. I reluctantly began to listen with my spirit rather than with my flesh. After all, she was an attractive, fine Christian woman— MAN (in Chris Tucker's voice)!" And soon afterward, the true purpose of her coming into my life finally sunk in. We would have godly conversations on the phone about this woman, and after our conversation was complete, in my best Doc Holliday voice, I sighed and said, "… and so she walks out of my life forever." Yep! She was gone—never to be seen again.

The time had come to meet this mystery woman and to forget "the woman I knew not!" I began to wonder, "What will this woman be like? How will she look?" Guys, you know what I'm saying! "Will she love God? Will she have children like me? If so, how will that work with my two? Can I love her like she needs to be loved? Can she give me what I need as a man?"

All of these questions came to mind as I embarked on a journey to find this woman of whom I had no knowledge. One thing was for certain, I had to trust God. I had to believe He would lead me to her because now, I truly believed she existed. I simply had to depend on God to bring her to me; and boy, did He ever!

As I have already mentioned, "inevitably God's Word

Chapter 3: The Meeting—28 Days

will come to pass on you—good or bad—it's coming to pass." Thank God, this was good. Patterns that had characterized my life had led me to this moment and time on my journey. "My good thing" was about to show up. Amazingly, God was aligning her to meet the purpose He had for her life as well. Nevertheless, He would cause us to collide peculiarly and incidentally, and that meeting would connect us for an eternity.

Oh, and one final thought on the woman who was obviously a precursor to this miraculous meeting with my destiny. I really thank God for her standing in the gap and never crossing the line with me. I mean, let's face it, we were two attractive people who were attracted to each other. Even though we had every opportunity as young adults, we never once overstepped our boundaries. I tried, but she never gave in; she was truly "the woman I knew not."

The Woman I Knew Not

Transcending down from heaven
Into her earthly form,
Sent especially for me—
She was profoundly borne.
She talked of things
That searched my depth,
Only to stir the gift within me.
And although I never knew her,
The way I felt, her having left,
I now know her presence was real.
As she whispered words of life
Into my fairly empty vessel—
Only to witness the overflow
After which she left.
And she left without saying goodbye
And with thanks I cried,
She was and will be
The woman I knew not.

Chapter 3: The Meeting—28 Days

Another Ministering Moment to Single Men

I want to take some pages to address single men. Oftentimes, because the Word of God says, "the man who finds a wife finds a good thing," we feel as though this verse somehow removes God from choosing our mate for us. Though we can find a wife, we must not seek to find her with our natural eyes. We must understand that God requires us through Scripture to:

> "Trust in the Lord with all thine heart, and lean not to thine own understanding; in all thy ways acknowledge him and he shall direct thy paths" (Proverbs 3:5, 6).

The Word of God also says in Psalm 37:4, "Delight thyself also in the Lord; and He will give you the desires of your heart.

Truly, my delight was practicing celibacy after the heartbreak of my previous marriage. I began learning through God, the epitome of a godly man. My relationship during this period gained momentum with the Lord as I patiently "waited on God" to lead me to my one true wife. "...He that is unmarried careth for the things that belong to the Lord, how he may please the Lord..." (1 Corinthians 7:32; KJV).

Notwithstanding, the Enemy devised a strategy to divert me through what I call "the season of the counterfeits."

The Counterfeits

In the season of the counterfeits, I met some animated characters while on my journey to meet my future wife. A lot of them would show up, but never the right one, so I kept searching. I met a young lady named Stephanie, and let me assure you, she was a character. I cannot say too much due to the graphic nature of the story; however, it would suffice to say she was not the one. Even though this aggressive, self-centered, provocative woman said she knew the Lord, everything but God was on her mind. She only wanted a bed partner. As you can imagine, that relationship ended before it began. (She was hot, fellas).

Continuing the voyage…I would soon meet yet another Stephanie, and I had to wonder "What's up with that?" Though on the surface, Stephanie II seemed like she had it all together, she was truly a vigorous character who could curse like a sailor and other things I cannot mention. All the same, she was an engineer and had a huge house and drove a nice car, but she was spiritually bankrupt. We had one date, and the beginning ended as quickly as it started. Both Stephanies were counterfeits, and I was beginning to think I would never find this woman.

Now I can return to telling the Holy Spirit, "Yeah, right" and my looking at the ceiling and all that. My family and I arrived at the skating rink, and there I noticed a woman who was absolutely beautiful. When she and I crossed paths, let me tell you, I thought she was breathtaking.

I was going and she was coming; it was as though time was in slow motion. Of course, I wanted to investigate further, but I had butterflies, so I asked my sister-in-law to go and ask her if she was with someone or if she was married. She did as I asked. All the while, I was trying to act like I wasn't watching, but I was. My sister-in-law asked her the questions and came back with all no's!

Remember, what the Holy Spirit had told me still hadn't dawned on me. I was in the moment; I was in swag mode. The kid was in full swing, and I knew it too; after all, I was that guy. I was so cool if the sun wasn't shining in a dark place, I still wore my shades. I finally mustered up enough courage to ask her name. My friend, guess what she said? Yes, her name was "Stephanie!" I couldn't believe what I heard! She was the third person in a row I had met by that name; nevertheless, I realized something was different about this Stephanie.

We talked and the conversation was great; shortly afterward, we exchanged numbers. I could feel that this woman was special. I noticed she had a different disposition about herself;

Chapter 3: The Meeting—28 Days

she spoke pleasantly, had a sweet spirit, and possessed a loveliness. Then I noticed she had two kids.

Let me stop here for a real moment: I can feel the sisters who are reading this thinking, "What do you mean 'she had kids'—especially when you have two of your own?" Before you go ballistic on me, please consider this: I was involved in a bad relationship experience that left me scarred. Though I prayed myself out of that hurt, I told the Lord I did not want a woman who had children. I truly thought that was best for me, and boy, was I totally wrong. Needless to say, God never answered that selfish prayer, and I am so thankful that He didn't! You see, oftentimes we feel we know what's best for us, but I'm glad to know that God knew me better than I knew myself.

When walking by faith, a person cannot see with his or her own eyes. This is supported by Scripture: "we walk by faith and not by sight." One might ask: "How does one see?" Oftentimes before working a miracle, Jesus asked, "Do you believe?" Here is where we find the answer. When you believe you exercise faith or when you have faith, you not only please God, but you grow to trust Him. When you trust Him, you see the situation as He does. I didn't know this truth at the time, but I was about to experience it.

Later that night, I noticed that I had a missed phone call and message, and behold, it was Stephanie—the woman I had just met at on Gospel skate night. She called a brother the same night?!! "What's really going on?" I wondered.

Stephanie's Account

Two days had passed since I had prayed a prayer to God concerning dating. I told the Lord that I did not want to meet another man unless He had sent him to be my husband. The last thing on my mind at this stage of my life was meeting someone because of that very personal prayer. On the night I met Kevin, I had promised my kids that I would take them skating after church—even though I wasn't feeling well. I wanted to keep my promise to them, so I took them anyway.

After arriving at the rink, I helped my daughter skate while my son played video games. Suddenly, this guy who was leaving the rink floor, passed me, and kept staring at me. I have to admit he was tall, dark, and handsome; I have to give him that. However, I couldn't help but notice he was wearing sunglasses inside the skating rink at night. My immediate thought was, "Who does that?"

Anyway, my daughter was thirsty, so I went to get her something to drink from the concession stand. We both sat down at a table to rest a little while. It was Gospel skate night, so the atmosphere was fairly low-key, and we were enjoying the music.

As I was resting a young lady approached me and said that her "anonymous" brother-in-law had sent her over to ask me if I was married. In my mind I was thinking, "Here we go again… As soon as I try to focus on God, here comes the Enemy with one of his players." I was so determined not to make the same mistakes I had made in the past. My heart was sincere, and my mind was made up.

Let's take a minute and pause in my telling of our meeting. I want to address the single ladies at this point in my story. I will never forget the time I was at church, listening to the preacher ministering on relationships. He said, "If you feel like it takes a man to complete you, then you are not ready for one."

As I have already mentioned, singleness is not only a time for preparation, it is also a time for developing your relationship with God. He wants to know that He is "the apple of your eye," that your life is centered around Him first, and that He can trust you to keep Him first. Remember, He is a jealous God in the sense that He isn't willing to share His glory with anyone else. He is deserving of all our attention, praise, honor and worship, and once He knows He has that from you, then He can trust you with His choice. The two of you can then serve Him together.

Chapter 3: The Meeting—28 Days

Waiting on God is so important!
Psalm 37:5 says, "Commit your way to the Lord, trust also in Him, and He shall bring it to pass."

Now back to the story at Gospel skate night... Even thought I was somewhat nonplussed by her question, I said, "No, I'm not married." Once he received that news, he came over. Wouldn't you know it? It was the guy with the sunglasses—"Kool Moe Dee." He told me his name was Kevin, and he went on to ask me more questions: "What do you do? How many kids do you have?" You know, he asked the usual stuff.

I thought the conversation went fairly well—for our first meeting. We talked for about ten minutes and decided to exchange numbers, then he departed. I allowed the kids to skate for another hour, and we left. Later that night, for some reason, I couldn't get him off my mind. I began debating about whether or not to call him. The number-one rule in dating for women is never to call first, or at least that had become the rule in my book. Nevertheless, I did the unthinkable, and I called him first. Luckily, since I did not want to be embarrassed, he didn't answer, so I left a message and went to bed.

Back to Kevin
The following day I called Stephanie, and we chatted the normal small talk filled with even more butterflies and uncased nervousness. I was at Six Flags over Georgia with my family, and I didn't have much time to talk. Before concluding the conversation, I uncommonly asked her to refer to me as "Poppie!"

Now ladies, before you pass the final judgment, and fellows before you high five me, please let me explain! Remember when I shared that I had, in fact, met two other Stephanies! Well, they were still calling me! Therefore, I needed a means to identify the ones I thought might be either of the counterfeits.

When she was hesitant, I explained to her that I needed a

way to filter out the other two Stephanies, ultimately leaving her as the last one standing. She consented with one condition: "In return, you must call me 'Mommie.'"

I happily agreed to her terms!

Later that night, something strange occurred, which I thought was uncommon for a so-called independent woman… she called! She explained that she was in the area and asked if I wanted something to eat, so I said, "Sure!" When she got to my house, we quickly ate our food and decided to take a stroll in the neighborhood.

We talked a great deal and became more acquainted with one another. At this point I was able to stare at her. Remember? I wore shades in the dark! Guys, I have to admit, right from the start I realized that I had hit the jackpot; she was the total package. She was spiritually beautiful on the inside, and on the outside, she was fine.

From that night and several days later, we talked and saw each other. I found our conversations so refreshing as they were all centered around the Word of God. She would listen to me talk for hours at a time without interrupting. She was teachable and humble—all qualities of a virtuous woman. We would visit each other's home church; hence, our first dates were in the house of God. We were having a great time. I knew God was up to something; I simply wasn't sure what. Everything about the situation felt so right.

Over the next few weeks, our times together became more fulfilling by the day. We noticed that we had so much in common. What stood out the most was our love for God. One week Stephanie's church was having a revival, and the preacher's subject addressed "In the beginning…" The man of God ministered about Adam and Eve in the beginning.

Every day of that particular week whether we were in church or listening to the radio, or watching TBN, the subject addressed "In the beginning." We questioned whether or not

Chapter 3: The Meeting—28 Days

God was trying to tell us something, and indeed, He was.

When we were riding in the car one day, the Holy Spirit spoke to us simultaneous, yet individually. "Get married!" We looked at one another, and said, "Let's get married!" I asked her, "Will you marry me?"

She said "Yes!"

On the twenty-eighth day of knowing one another, in obedience to God, we were married. Can you believe it, people? In only 28 days, we were married!! I finally saw what God wanted me to see. This indeed was my wife!

I was so thankful that the Lord had led me in finding my "good thing." I realized that our courtship was exactly like "The Woman I Knew Not" had said! What a true testament to the importance of waiting on God for Stephanie, as well as for myself. God brought us to the ultimate place of being joined together to meet the complete purpose that He had for our lives.

Through all the counterfeits, through patience, through committing to a life of celibacy, through persistence in prayer, through consistently and faithfully going to service, I finally met my good half—the person in the beginning of this story to whom I was conjoined, but was separated, only to allow God to bring us back together in His timing.

My friend, can't you see what we're trying to say to you? The purpose of God through waiting, or serving Him, and allowing Him to afflict you will ultimately bring you into His plan and perfect will for your life. In spite of how it began, the end of this particular matter came full circle. Such was the case for us. Now the becoming one was vastly approaching, and nothing we could have done could have prepared us for what was coming by the proving of God through more increased affliction.

WAITING ON GOD

Chapter 4:
Two Becoming One— The Truth

AFTER CAREFULLY CONSIDERING THE SERIOUS ramifications of what I am about to share, I have concluded that not only is it necessary, but fundamental, to believers who are in Christ Jesus. It is imperative that we as Christians retain understanding and wisdom. As I have previously stated, they are "the principle thing."

While taking time to relax one day and watch some television, I became aware of an emerging pattern. I noticed that almost every commercial I had seen that day was filled with hidden innuendos to subliminally permeate the minds of viewers. I personally witnessed the imputation of deceitfulness, designed to redirect and to rid humanity of the God ordained order He had given to man. The commercials were constantly showing women as the dominant force over man. These men willingly subjected themselves for the sake of avoiding some sort of punishment that would follow if they did not comply. They portrayed the woman as having authority over a truly submissive, fragile, docile man.

Every reader knows what I am addressing! "If you don't do what she says, you have to sleep on the couch." Who can forget the statement, "She's always right?" Or the classic one: she can hit you and do almost anything to you, but if you somehow harm her, you automatically go to jail. "After all, a man should never hit a woman."

By the way, I do not advocate men striking women any more than I promote women hitting men. I find all of this brutality and impropriety far from the intent of God concerning relationships between men and women—let alone married couples. The Bible is clear and decisive in its rendering from God to mankind.

In the book of Genesis, the Fall of mankind came through the disobedience of one man—Adam. This indictment on man, however, does not in any way suggest that the woman was somehow innocent, According to the Word of God, she was the one deceived. Of course, judgments were given by God for these sinful acts to both parties involved in Genesis 3:14-17:

> "And the Lord God said unto the woman, what is this that thou hast done? And the woman said, the serpent beguiled me, and I did eat. And the Lord God said unto the serpent, Because thou hast done this, thou art cursed above all cattle, and above every beast of the field; upon thy belly shalt thou go, and dust shalt thou eat all the days of thy life: And I will put enmity between thee and the woman, and between thy seed and her seed; it shall bruise thy head, and thou shalt bruise his heel. Unto the woman he said, I will greatly multiply thy sorrow and thy conception; in sorrow thou shalt bring forth children; and thy desire shall be to thy husband, and he shall rule over thee. And unto Adam he said, because thou hast hearkened unto the voice of thy wife, and hast eaten of the tree, of which I commanded thee, saying, Thou shalt not eat of it: cursed is the ground for thy sake; in sorrow shalt thou eat of it all the days of thy life."

Chapter 4: Two Becoming One—The Truth

I dare not state the obvious that seemingly no one in the church or the rest of the world for that matter are willing to say or teach. First, God came to man and asked … "Where art thou?" (v. 9) It is important to point out that God knew exactly where the man was, but He was simply trying to show man his fallen state, and make him realize and admit his sin. Adam then directs God's attention toward Eve (his wife) and says, "The woman whom thou gavest to be with me, she gave me of the tree, and I did eat" (v. 12).

I have heard many messages preached in churches that would suggest that the blame totally fell on Adam and that Eve was somehow the victim. A careful study of Scripture reveals that was far from the truth by reason of what follows in verse 13.

And the Lord God said unto the woman, "What is this that thou hast done?…"

The woman then passes the guilt to the serpent, and the charges ceased. God immediately passes judgment on the serpent, judgment on Eve follows and finally Adam. Notice the chain of events pertaining to punishments from least (the serpent) to greatest (both Adam and his wife as they are one). God's love for mankind is immense, and for that reason, this is why what followed had to take place in order to set matters right.

Judgment came to the woman because she listened to the serpent and not her husband. Judgment came to the man because he listened to his wife and not the command of God. A pattern emerged from the beginning that still exists to this day; i.e., man is constantly hearkening to everyone else instead of God. This lack of respect for God's commands, which is what caused His judgment upon the earth, today causes marriages to fail. Satan used Eve to get to Adam because Adam had direct orders from God. Eve was the closest person to Adam as the two were one flesh. She was his weaker part, and she was the one who provided the serpent (Satan) a way to destroy the will of God through Adam.

In today's society, the woman has been exalted back into this role, which is a direct ploy of Satan's to undermine the authority of man given by God, as well as to set things in order in the earth, the family and the church. This, of course, would put man back into the driver's seat with a huge responsibility; nonetheless, the woman would not be so easily persuaded. I am referring to Genesis 3:16, in which God said the following to Eve:

"Thy desire shall be to thy husband, and he shall rule over thee."

The word desire in the Hebrew text means: "stretching out after, a yearning, a longing, a desire." The word appears only three times in the Old Testament, and twice the word refers to the strong attraction between the genders. One of these two times is in the context of love and joy (Song of Solomon 7:10), and the other is in the context of sin and judgment (Genesis 3:16). The third passage describes personified sin as being like a crouching animal ready to pounce on Cain (Genesis 4:7).

The woman would possess a strong, sincere attraction toward her husband, but this judgment still was not a joyous occasion. Like God used this word desire in the case of Adam and Eve, the full meaning in its usage can be found in Genesis 4:5-7 when God addressed Cain concerning his brother Abel:

> "But unto Cain and to his offering he had not respect. And Cain was very wroth, and his countenance fell. And the Lord said unto Cain, Why art thou wroth? And why is thy countenance fallen? If thou doest well, shalt thou not be accepted? And if thou doest not well, sin lieth at the door. And unto thee shall be his desire, and thou shalt rule over him. ...Cain rose up against his brother and slew him." KJV

Because God had put the man over the woman, she, like Cain, would rise up (have no respect), and her desire [shall be against]

Chapter 4: Two Becoming One—The Truth

this divine order as society (sin) has taught women to be insubordinate to this truth. Crouching at the very thought of a man having rule over her, this divine order would not be easily received by women.

My wife and I had to comply with this truth by being examples of the Gospel; and as you can imagine, following God's divine order was not easy for either of us. We had many years of secularization that had demoralized God's view of marriage.

God has a divine order in His kingdom that all must observe and obey. The Bible tells us that the man is God's glory, and the woman is man's glory.

> "The man is the image and the glory of God, and the woman is the glory of the man. She was created for the man and not the man for her. For this cause ought the woman to have power on her head because of angels. He is her covering! He is over her!" (1 Corinthians 11:7-11)

This divine order applies not only to mankind, but also to the heavenly host; they too have an order and are subordinate to one another.

My wife and I were about to find out exactly what God had envisioned for our marriage, having already established a blueprint called order. I first had to learn how to obey God and to lead, to love, to honor, to provide and to protect. She had to learn how to submit, to love, to obey, not to usurp authority over me, and to walk as a virtuous woman. The Lord was and is our Mediator, our Referee. He was the One Who kept us from error.

The Fairy Tale

When two people meet and fall in love, next comes the wedding with all of the trimmings—you know, the big American dream. A wedding with all of the trimmings is the fantasy not only of those in the secular arena but also for those in the church. I'll admit, it sounds great, but only if it really happens that way. So what I am about to share will sound crazy to some and shocking to others. Okay, here goes…

My wife and I got married twenty-eight days after we met; however, we were NOT IN LOVE! She will be the first to admit the truth of this declaration. I know, I know…some of you are thinking, how can you marry someone with whom you are not in love? Although what happened to my wife and me was not the "norm," it was actually sound.

My wife and I married out of obedience to God. By faith we believed that everything else would follow. Let me state for the record that I love my wife very much; she is my "good thing"; however, loving each another didn't happen for us overnight. In fact, if you are really honest with yourself, it didn't happen overnight for you.

Many things occurred with my wife and me in the beginning of our marriage. Seemingly right "out of the gate," our union would be tested. Neither of us really had any indication of what we were getting into. In our culture today, everyone wants the "fairytale" dream wedding, and nothing is wrong with that desire. On the other hand, we simply don't calculate the sacrifice it takes in obtaining a successful marriage.

Many churches have adopted the process of pre-marital counseling, but few ever master the progression. They fail to break down individual preconceived ideas of what each person thinks marriage is. Repeatedly, society dictates to us the marital plan, rather than bearing in mind matrimony through the eyes of God.

Genesis 2:18 says: "And the Lord God said, "It is not good that man should be alone; I will make him a helper comparable to him" (NKJV). The word help meet as it is written in the King James Version means "counterpart or mate" in the Hebrew language. This meaning is interesting because God made Eve from Adam's rib, out of his side. The word meet describes woman as man's counterpart in marriage. In Webster's Dictionary, the word counterpart means "one of two parts that fit, complete, or complement one another."

The Word of God says in Genesis 2:24, "Therefore a man shall leave his father and mother and be joined to his wife, and the two shall become one flesh."

Our Story: The Not-So Fairytale
On October 20, 2000, I was married to my "good thing"—Stephanie—you know, the one from whom I was separated before my birth. Did I really marry someone I had only known for a month? We had asked each other, knowing we were both thinking about marriage. To add to the delight, I must share that I was on leave from my job. When we look back on our wedding day and our marriage, we now know that it was all God. After so much joy and spiritual bliss for almost a month, reality was now beginning to settle in.

We equally had all kinds of emotions we were dealing with internally, praying we had not made a huge mistake. I was starting to have some doubts due to the soul ties still lurking on the inside of me. I longed to be with my kids; I had always promised that I would rear them in my own house and be a big part of their lives—especially since I did not grow up with my biological father. Not being able to be with them was one consequence of my having them in haste. The residue of their mother's and my relationship haunted me—in the sense that I felt guilty and torn for not having my children with me. My heartache wasn't that I still wanted to be with their mother because I knew she wasn't the wife God had for me; however, my desire to rear my kids was worth my settling for their good. Not having my children with me was becoming very difficult. I did not calculate the ramifications of another man's rearing them in my place. Even though I wasn't reared by my father, the emerging pattern was clear to me.

Satan knows the exact way to snare us; and he was hot on

my trail, using my children. My wife began noticing I would act somewhat strange whenever my children came to visit, and also when I talked to their mother. Stephanie suspected I still had feelings for my ex-girlfriend. Can you imagine the confusion and pain I felt that was affecting my wife? I was becoming an emotional wreck. Battling within myself, I finally shared my feelings with my wife. I knew it was hard for Stephanie to understand, but I knew I had to be completely honest with her. I explained to her what little I understood about my feelings at that moment. What I was about to share with her was undeniably complex; and if she did not hear my explanation with a spiritual ear, we would surely divorce. I knew I had to seek God for the rest.

I can discern what you are thinking. You are saying, "You didn't want to be with another woman?" No! "You weren't having feelings for another woman?" No! That's the world's way of thinking. Many people never take the time to go past what I call "surface feelings." We only see the understandable and never search for what lies beneath—the matters which are spiritual.

Allow me to share an example: when Jesus was being crucified, the persons calling for His death could not see the spiritual implications of the act they were taking part in performing. We know this because Jesus allows us to see their ignorance in His following statement: "Father forgive them for they know not what they do." These Roman soldiers only knew what they saw and understood—not what was spiritual like Christ. I had to explain this fact to my wife; it wasn't what the Enemy was trying to project, it had a deeper spiritual meaning.

We were at church one night, and a woman evangelist was ministering. She spotted us in the crowd and called us forward because she had a word of prophecy from the Lord:
"God told me to tell you two to spend as much time together as you can because the Enemy will to try to separate you!"
Remember what I wrote in the beginning of the book? I was separated from my counterpart; obviously, the Adversary did not

Chapter 4: Two Becoming One—The Truth

want us together.

Up until this service, we had never before seen this woman evangelist, so we knew the word she spoke was from God. In all actuality, from ministry to ministry we were experiencing this type of word everywhere we went. I guess these "words" were God's way of confirming our marriage because He knew some rocky days were ahead, and those were the times when we would question if our marriage was really in His will. He had put us together for ministry, and that would be our saving grace. God knew this truth about us—even though we did not have an inkling of the total spiritual understanding. This is why I constantly affirmed myself to my wife. The Enemy was after my marriage using the outside forces of the weakness I had for my children and finances. The importance of "waiting on God" is also the importance of "seeking God."

> "Let no man deceive himself; if any man among you seemeth to be wise in this world, let him become a fool, that he may be wise" (1 Corinthians 3:18; KJV).

> "For the natural man receives not the things of the Spirit of God: for they are foolishness unto him: neither can he know them, because they are spiritually discerned. But he that is spiritual judges all things, yet he himself is judged of no man" (1 Corinthians 2:14, 15).

We were on a spiritual expedition, exploring our all-knowing, wise God. Having a successful marriage would take our believing in Him, trying not to be deceived, judging all things spiritually while obeying Him, and hoping our faith would lead us on.

So we spent all of our time together as instructed. We wanted to learn more about our past as we made plans for the future. At that time, I was on leave from my job due to mental distress.

Did you commit to memory the statement—"Forget what you have been told or think you know about God"—I made at the very beginning? Well, one night when I was walking home from work, the Holy Spirit said to me, "You're about to be robbed." I immediately dismissed the warning and kept walking. (You would have thought I knew the voice of God by now.) But I did and I didn't know His voice. Soon after my mental deficiency and act of ignorance, the inevitable happened exactly as God had said.

What I'm about to share is rather chilling. However, assuredly it is so important for every believer to know the voice of God and to obey Him when you hear Him.

> "Never consider what God didn't say; only obey what He says."—Kevin L. Lipsey, Sr.

Of course, I learned this truth the hard way—as I later pondered not only if my experience was God, but also why would He allow me to be robbed.

I ignored the nudging of the Holy Spirit, and suddenly a silver-polished, nickel-plated 9mm was pointed right between my eyes. My immediate thought was, "I can't believe this is happening to me!" Nothing you will ever imagine can prepare you for a defining moment such as this. Satan himself tried to impede my life by ending it, but God would prove not only to be all-knowing, but all powerful in this situation. The Lord gave me insight on the enemy's plight to destroy my life. Although I didn't hearken to His voice, all things worked together for the good.

After the unknown, visibly advantaged man unexpectedly rolled up on me, he told me to get down on the ground, but I refused. I must say, please don't do what I did under any circumstances—unless you are seriously hearing from God. Anyway, af-

Chapter 4: Two Becoming One—The Truth

ter my unwillingness to cooperate; he started asking if I had any money on my person. Thankfully, I had been paid and was able to give him what he asked. When he got the money, he jumped in the car and left. I was so relieved.

Afterward, I made it to where I was staying when a man approached me because he had seen the entire robbery. He proceeded to call the police, and I asked him not to. Then I began to witness to him and asked if he knew Christ.

What? I had just been robbed at gunpoint and was asking someone if he knew Christ. Now you know why I was on leave when I met and married my wife, but let me conclude the matter because this robbery played a significant role in my marriage or what we think marriage should be.

I thought I was okay after the robbery, but I later discovered that I was actually traumatized. The effects of the trauma did not show up right away, but weeks later, the effects of being held at gunpoint finally got to me mentally. The pain was terrible to deal with, and so many nights I pondered, "Why me, Lord?" I had thought if I could simply testify in church about how the Lord had rescued me, that I would be able to move on, but what I believed proved untrue. I was seriously troubled by the experience.

Yes, we overcome the Adversary by the word of our testimony, but someone forgot to tell me that it would take some serious time. For me, the recovery took a whole lot of time—so much that the trauma of the incident quickly began affecting me at my job. Eventually I was told by my district manager that I had become ineffective at my job. "For your good," he said, "I am placing you on leave and sending you home." But the story doesn't end here.

Before this incident occurred, while I was at another job, God had spoken to me that He did not want me at this job. This fact was later confirmed by a pastor who also heard from God two weeks prior to God telling me. When it was told to me in church one night, the congregation marveled! The pastor immediately rebuked the people and told them not to be in awe because they would not be able to handle what God would allow me to go through. Unknown to me at the time, the robbery was suddenly clear. Man tends to listen to everyone except God. Every believer has to learn how to obey the Heavenly Father, and sometimes we have to learn the hard way.

In spite of what I thought, being robbed brought me to where God wanted me to be. He had never intended to harm me; rather, His desire was to move me in obedience.

I find it so interesting how God can reveal something great about your life or allow greatness to enter your life, and then suddenly a drastic change occurs. My life was starting to take a turn for the better. I had met and married my "good thing," and then God says, "I don't want you on a man's job!"

I was like "What? How can I support my family? I don't understand! What will she think of me? Or worse yet, what will people think of me?" Don't misunderstand, I want to be obedient, but I didn't want to disappoint my new wife. Nevertheless, I knew the Bible says that obeying is better than sacrifice.

I am reminded of the story of Joseph in the Bible. Most people know the story of how God had revealed to Joseph through dreams that God would make him great and that he would lead his brothers. Not long after this revelation, his brothers' jealous would lead them to cast Joseph into a pit. Their jealousy did not stop there; they sold younger brother into slavery, he was taken to Egypt, falsely accused of rape and sent to prison for many, many years before the dream would be fulfilled (Genesis 37-47). In some ways, I felt a little like Joseph. My life was beginning to unfold much like his.

> "Greatness was the expected end; however, afflictions were to come first."—Kevin L. Lipsey, Sr.

Chapter 4: Two Becoming One—The Truth

Though I obeyed God in getting married, and my wife and I were in one accord; as time went on, I found it was becoming even more difficult to obey God and please my wife and family. I also needed a job. Through many attempts and many job failures, God proved that He was not budging from His intentions concerning me; eventually, I would have to surrender. If I would be obedient, then I would come into my fullness; but if I didn't; my wife and my family would continue to escape the promise. My future and their futures were in God's hands through His using me. You know, like Moses and the children of Israel.

Allow me to share a thought from part one of one of my messages entitled, "Acquainted with Grief":
"When confronted with the difficulties and complexities of life, most of us would rather avoid the very notion of suffering—shunning the idea that God would allow such atrocities in our lives...."

Most of us would, at all costs, desperately try to escape the thing God is using to promote us or by teaching us His ways that we may be usable in His kingdom. This is exactly what God was doing with me and my wife. We would have to minister this very lesson to many believers one day in the future, but then that inescapable question kept coming up to the both of us: "Why me?"

What Good Is Good?

I say then what good is good? When you're out of the inner
Dwelling in that place where one shouldn't—
in the company of the sinner?
Not to stand as a witness, one tries to convince
And so he goes on like nothing is wrong; it doesn't make sense.
What good is it? When you're not where God wants you to be,
You're out of the will, and so your spirit can't receive.
What good is it? When your good is fame
To learn what's it all for? It was truly vain.
I looked around to see where I now stand
Only to find that where I stand is not where I once stood
Trying to do something, Hmmm…
What good is your good?

Chapter 4: Two Becoming One—The Truth

As I surrendered to God, He began working on spiritually piecing my wife and me together. We submerged ourselves into the Word of God through intense studies, with midnight and early morning prayers and fasting. We were on a spiritual sabbatical. God was taking His time to develop our relationship while casting down every wall of modern-day society definition of marriage. God began showing us that He alone was sovereign, and that He had the right to do whatever He desired to do with our marriage. What God was revealing to us through Scripture was coming up against everything we had been previously taught. We saw ourselves in the midst of the Scriptures and noticed that we were on the wrong side of the Word. God was taking us against the grain, which we now recognize as His "more excellent way." This seeking of God, however, led to many changes in our marriage as well as our household. We turned to the painstaking task of blending a family. We didn't know taking all of these God-ordained steps would become the preparation for our ministry in the kingdom.

Blending the Family

To blend means "to combine or mix so that the constituent parts are indistinguishable from one another; a harmonious assimilation resulting from an occurrence of thorough mixing." Both my wife and I, who had grown up with stepfathers, had experienced being a part of a fused family. Contrary to what we have shared, we continue to respect and appreciate the sacrifices our stepfathers made in their efforts in this synthesis. We were familiar with certain aspects of amalgamation, but nothing could prepare us for the type of fusion my wife and I had to face.

I particularly enjoy the play of words previously displayed in the last paragraph. Though they all mean relatively the same thing, they somehow provide us with a more detailed view of the process of blending a family.

These procedures require highly skilled individuals in

the areas of the Word and one who constantly hears from God. Stephanie and I were obviously not these people. Although we did however, have the Lord God on our side. My friend, we were only married about a year by this time, but now a new test, "blending a family." So we decided, "Let's do this!"

Through centuries many have seen and heard of the kindness of one to another when it comes to rearing a child not of his or her blood. Many great stories exist, I'm sure; however, one particular paramount story, in my mind, supersedes the rest. The story of Joseph and Mary oftentimes receives little attention to the fact that theirs was truly a fusion. This good man reared a child from his wife's womb, but nowhere from his loins and not to mention his bloodline and didn't feel shame, embarrassment, remorse, awkward nor humiliated about Jesus.

This was the ultimate blended family, if you will, because Christ is the child in question. Can you imagine Joseph's thoughts? I wonder if Joseph and Mary might have had the same problems my wife and I had. I am relatively sure God the Father was not jealous and did not cause problems for Joseph and Mary. I wonder if Mary told her husband when he spanked the little boy Jesus, "You're being too hard on him!" I wonder, did they ever have arguments? Did she throw up in his face: "This is not your child"? Was Joseph apprehensive in disciplining Jesus because of that possibility? Oh, we can't forget this one: I wonder how Joseph felt about loving and caring for a child who wasn't his own. These are thoughts and questions that make you go hmmmm!!!

Although we have no way of knowing the answers to these questions, I am sure the same applies to us today, and most certainly to me and mine. Yes, we had to address these serious marriage-breaking problems, and facing the issues was not simple. Together, my wife and I have four children—two are my biological children, and two are her biological children. Together we are like "the Brady Bunch!"

Chapter 4: Two Becoming One—The Truth

In our blended family, I am thankful to say that the four kids got along just fine; the adults on both sides of the spectrum became the real issue. We weren't only dealing with the other fathers and mothers, but we also had to address an "in-house battle between the Mrs. and the Mr." Problems arise when your past is not resolved; you cannot really move forward until they are. This was happening in our case with the assimilation of our family. I still had to address "residue" from my previous relationship with my children's mother. Our unresolved issues, which dictated the way we handled the children, also added to the circumstances in my household.

These other people outside of the marriage did not want us to discipline each other's children when they were at our house. Demands like these are sure to keep a family from becoming one. They seek to inject the family with outside control, and you cannot effectively manage your household, especially when trying to rear the children according to the Word of God. Oftentimes, my children's biological mother and I did not agree when it came to correction; as a result, we were constantly at each other's throats. She obviously had more control due to the fact that the kids lived with her, which allowed her to dictate what I could or could not do concerning them. I only wanted to do right by them; after all, they were my seed. Because of this constant turmoil, my desire for my children to be with me grew even stronger.

However, I realized they were also her kids, and I am quite sure she was doing what she thought was right. I also realized I was paying the consequences of my past decisions. A pattern that characterizes a person's life was now making its way into my children's life. Through a great deal of pain and time spent in prayer, I came to the conclusion that I could not be a full-time father in another household (a consequence of my not waiting on God).

I was devastated because I would have little-to-no influence in my children's lives. I knew I had to find some common ground. I had no other choice but to rely on the Lord for help and strength. I had never been in a situation like this one, and more would soon follow.

Lessons Learned

The other side of the spectrum was in the area of dealing with the fathers of Stephanie's children. Her son's father and I got along quite nicely, probably due to our mutual respect for one another. Her daughter's father, on the other hand, was altogether different. He personally had a problem with our marital union and with me. He had expressed to me that he did not want me disciplining his daughter in any way, and I saw his interference as an attempt to control my household.

My wife was also embracing a great deal of anger concerning her daughter's father. This anger was the result of the fact that their separation wasn't peaceful on his part, as well as his failure to provide for his child. I can recall engaging in a conversation with my wife one day as she was venting over a letter from the child support agency. This letter stated that her ex-husband had not made a payment in over a year, and a tone of revenge ensued. His deep animosity toward Stephanie led her to harbor her own anger. This anger had obviously resulted from previous relationships, especially when it came to disciplining her children.

Whenever the subject would come up, all of this rage would come out of her. Finally I discerned by the Spirit of God that she had some internal issues she had not addressed. She was harboring un-forgiveness in her heart. When I first confronted her about this matter, her first reaction was to deny it and scold me for thinking such a thing. However, as I persisted in speaking the Word of God, she relented. Consequently, by searching her heart, she discovered that I was correct in my assessment.

Even though this man did not care for me, I instructed my wife to release him from child support. After all, he wasn't paying it anyway. I told her maybe he couldn't pay it at this time, and that God was her source—not man.

Chapter 4: Two Becoming One—The Truth

The Lord says that "Vengeance is mine," and the Spirit showed me that it wasn't her place to make someone pay for something she felt was wrong—even if it was legitimate. I could speak on this matter because I had been placed in the same situation with my children's mother.

Even though Stephanie's ex-husband did not care for me, I believe I understood his stance, and I honestly did not want another man to feel what I had felt. I did not want him to be told what to do by the system. Since God didn't want me on a man's job, he would have to provide for my children supernaturally, and now for my wife's daughter. God proved his watch care to me by touching the heart of my children's mother, prompting her to remove me from the child support system. To my amazement, and like the Scripture promised, my children have never had to beg for bread. I love my children, and I am sure the father of Stephanie's daughter did too, but he did not need anyone else to convey that to him.

Real love manifests in several different ways, depending upon the person who is giving that specific affection. I can honestly believe that my stepdaughter's father loved her in his own way, in a way that Stephanie could not detect. Likewise, Stephanie loved her daughter as well, but in a way he could not understand. In the eyes of Stephanie's love, she felt child support would help reveal the love she wanted him to have for his daughter and thereby prove his love for his child. However, the way he loved said, "I don't have the finances at the moment, so I'll prove my love by trying to spend time with my daughter." Either way, both loved their daughter in their own way, but in opposition to one another. As you will see, God was the final authority in deciding this dispute. However, paying for children will never replace the importance of a father's rearing his kids. A good man does not have to be told to take care of his children's needs. The Bible says in Matthew 7:9, "Or what man is there of you, whom if his son ask for bread, will he give a stone?"

God loves us with a perfect love. I did not see this truth at the time, but I was doing unto others as I would have them to do unto me. Following this principle reminds me of something the Holy Spirit revealed to me concerning fathers.

Abba Father

The Holy Spirit suddenly revealed to me that one of the biggest misconceptions concerning fathers is how important they are to the family. Too often in this society much of the focus is on the mother, and even though she plays an important part in the rearing of their offspring, fathers are equally as important and possibly even more so.

Consider the Catholic church and how Mary, the mother of Jesus, is worshipped. While it is true that Christ was born of her, His Heavenly Father is clearly overlooked. Why worship someone Christ Himself did not worship? Jesus gave all the glory to the Father, from Whom He came. His entire identity came from His Heavenly Father.

The Father gave His Son life and purpose. Christ proclaimed in Scripture that He came to do the will of Him Who had sent Him (His Father). Why does society worship women as though they are goddesses, and why are fathers generally overlooked? No one person should be worshipped other than the true living God, but an imbalance clearly exists that needs restoring.

On the whole, men have lost influence over their families, their purpose, their children, their wives, and even the church. Therefore, we go on perpetuating these ideologies we have created. That little boy or girl who simply needs a father must take a backseat because we dare admit that we, as a society, got it wrong. So they grow up without a father's guidance, his leadership, his correction, his protection, his security and stability. Sure that their children do not need these intangibles, he thinks, "I'll just give them the money." We need "Abba Father!"

To the surprise of Stephanie's ex, she released him from

Chapter 4: Two Becoming One—The Truth

paying child support and simply told him to help her with their daughter when he could. This step allowed him to release the hatred in his heart; and accordingly, he began providing and spending more time with his daughter simply because he felt a sense of release. Glory to God!

Let me show you how God works! Within that year, Stephanie's ex-husband would pass away; my stepdaughter's father was gone. If Stephanie had not released him from paying child support, he would have left this world with un-forgiveness in his heart, and his daughter would not have had the opportunity to bond with her dad before his departure from this world. Only God could see the big picture.

For unknown reasons like this, it is so important to be obedient to the voice of God and not show partiality to others in spite of how they feel toward you. This life-changing event was a hard, sad lesson for our family. Waiting (obeying) on God is so important. We had no way of knowing at the beginning of the relationship that the outcome would culminate in this way. However, walking by faith and learning to patiently trust God would see us through.

The Regulation of the Household

After dealing with outside issues which lasted longer than any of us would have liked, the time had come to set things in order within my own house. This desire would difficult because the outside influences had left serious residue that reaped havoc.

We received divisive dictates about how to discipline the children, and we both viewed each other doing so. I will admit that the blueprint was obviously there through the Word of God, but the totality of trust somehow evaded us. Remember the questions about Joseph, Mary and Jesus? We were now faced with the reality of those same questions that went unanswered, which forced us to dig deep for the solution.

My wife's previous relationships (but not her ex-husband)

had left her tainted when it came to allowing men to discipline her children. This view, of course, posed a problem because I was a disciplinarian by right; however, that had to take a backseat as I would have to humble myself in gaining my wife's trust. Before enforcing my rules, I would have to do a great deal of praying because my wife was hovering over everything I did in regard to her kids. She wanted to make sure that they were safe, and she also wanted me to be fair in my disciplining of all of the kids. I will tell you this was a very difficult process.

We were not as yet operating as a unified family; thus, we still had to face some issues of "hers" versus "mine' and vice versa. This polarity led to many arguments and disagreements; but again, we had the blueprint. My wife wanted her way, and I wanted my way, but we had to explore what God was saying. What was He doing in our family? Why was He stretching us, forcing us to see things as He saw them? Well, I can tell you that these times were painful, though they were for our good.

To our women readers, I know you may not like or you may completely disagree with what I am about to say, but as my wife will tell you, it's certainly true. Only one person can lead a household, and the only way that a reasonable resolve will be reached was our first consulting and following the Word of God. In order for us to hear from God on this particular matter, we had to submit ourselves one to another. Let's be perfectly clear: I am not talking about mutual submission, for the Bible does not teach this. My wife had to learn not only to submit under my headship in the home, but she had to also trust God that she had a man of God who would love her and would not hurt her children.

As a man of God, I had to be able to hear from God and convince her of my loyalty to God. This released the peace of God that surpasses all understanding. When we obey God, He can release wisdom and understanding. For it is written in I Corinthians 1:19-20,

Chapter 4: Two Becoming One—The Truth

"...I will destroy the wisdom of the wise, and will bring to nothing the understanding of the prudent. Where is the wise? Where is the scribe? Where is the disputer of this world? Hath not God made foolish the wisdom of this world?"

The answer is yes. Who can dispute? Who is wiser than God? Society would suggest that everyone is entitled to feel any way he pleases concerning his own children; however, God's ways are far higher than the way of the world. The answer was already there; we simply had to line up and ask God for wisdom. Feelings and emotions play a huge part in these sensitive areas. That's why we have to turn to the wisdom and order of God. The Bible indeed commands us what to do.

The husband is the head, and he answers to God; the wife honors God by submitting and honoring her husband. Next, the children are to obey their parents, thereby forming a three-string cord, knitted together like unto the Father, the Son, and the Holy Spirit. This, my friends is the core of blending a family.

My wife and I were now committed. We had embarked on a journey, and we had come too far to turn back now. We knew enough about God that if we left the relationship, the divorce would have enormous implications. We realized that lives were at stake, and we, along with God, were intertwined—if we had only known why.

Allow me to share another thought from part two of one of my messages entitled, "Acquainted with Grief":

> But to understand Christ in the lowly place is to comprehend the place selected by God that we may commune with Him, learn of Him, and die to the flesh—all while God plots our elevation and promotion—however demanding that you convey to those who witness your com-

ing out, the experiences you had with God....

Why Me?

That is the question—the inclination
I arrived to after the experience
came from within, out!

It didn't make sense that the question asked
couldn't be answered except you go through,
then you arrive!

I am there—here in that dark place
unable to retain my feelings, yet I feel them around me
Why me? Why?

I cry aloud only to hear no answer, but I can feel them.
It's cold and dark; I can't see my way.
The answers are there, but I can't see them!
Now it's time, I must pray.

WAITING ON GOD

Chapter 5:
Cast Out, But Not Destroy— Satan's Plot

When taking into consideration the fact that our universe, our solar system, and everything that exists—seen or unseen—was created by the Creator, how can anyone assume the position of being in control of his own destiny? The more knowledge you receive from God and the more you comprehend His Sovereignty in all His greatness, you will come to realize you do not have control at all. That is the highest place of understanding anyone can have.

Allow me to share another thought from my message entitled, "Acquainted with Grief":

> Meekness toward God is that disposition of spirit in which we accept His dealings with us as good, and therefore, without disputing or resisting. Thus, meekness toward evil people means knowing God is permitting the injuries they inflict, that He is using them to purify His elect, and that He will deliver His elect in His time (Isaiah 41:17, Luke 18:1-8, Philippians 1:29).
>
> Every person must remember that he was bought with a

price, and he no longer belongs to himself. If you are born again, Jesus becomes your Master, and you become His servant. Accepting this role positions you as a huge threat against the powers of darkness, which will thereby open you to direct hits from Satan as he exercise plots to destroy you. But my friend, don't be dismayed!

The Word declares that the weapon may be formed, but it shall not prosper. Jesus has already equipped all believers with the tools that are needed to overcome the Enemy. The Word of God is our sword and shield. Every attempt of the Enemy will surely fail. In this chapter and others, we will unveil Satan's ploy to take us out of ministry for good. We will address how God would establish me as a proponent of correction and truth. We will journey through time and seasons of ups and downs, twist and turns. So hold on to your seats as we explore God's strategic plan to usher us into our destiny, even as we traveled through the pitfalls of life.

At this writing, my wife and I had now been married for about a year, and we were finally starting to mesh together as a family unit. Things were getting tough in our personal life, but they were good in ministry. God was also starting to pour more deeply and intimately into us. In fact, I am reminded of one of my wife's clients.

An older man, who was a bishop of several churches, came to our salon to get his hair shampooed and cut by my wife. One day he invited us to visit his church for a service and then ministered a profound word—one that would change us for the rest of our life. The experience was tremendous! He looked as though he was in his prime, but his looks did not make the lasting impression. The bishop's entire sermon was about Jesus, Jesus, and more Jesus! He preached Jesus crucified, risen, His majesty, His Spirit, His Lordship and everything else in between. By the time we left, we realized that all of our days in church and ministry was all summed up to that one name: "Jesus!"

Chapter 5: Cast Out, But Not Destroyed—Satan's Plot

It's safe to say that the veil came off our eyes that day, and we were indeed enlightened. After hearing his sermon, we began intense word studies in view of Jesus' being there from Genesis to Revelation. Soon we would discover that Jesus was "concealed" in the Old Testament; in the New Testament, He was "revealed."

He was there the whole time. We had always known of Jesus, but now God was enlightening Him to us in a more personal way that has catapulted us into areas we never dreamed. With this new understanding of what this whole thing was really about, I had to re-evaluate everything I had been taught about the Word of God. I started to discover the flaws and erroneous teachings that were being preached about Christ. Before being enlightened, I would agree with much of what I had heard, but now all that I thought I knew did not sit well with my spirit. My wife and I thought we were going crazy because where we were once with the majority, we were now in the minority. To be honest, I felt like it was us against the world, and our journey was only beginning.

> "Persecution can cause either growth or bitterness in the Christian life. Our response determines the result." – Kevin L. Lipsey, Sr.

In our newfound wisdom and understanding, we came up against the order of that day. We were about to see that wisdom and understanding came with a price. We were persecuted and thrown out of churches for revealing the truth already revealed. Our personal lives were in chaos. We became homeless and were forced to live in a hotel, we would battle sickness and disease, and the list goes on.

Going Back; How It All Began

Have you ever been in a situation where all the people ever did was to put you out of a place? To them, it didn't matter whether or not it was hot or cold, good or bad. I cannot imagine when any time is a good time to put someone out of a place for no apparent reason. The feeling of rejection, loneliness, and the lack of compassion that comes is incredible to embrace. What would possess a person to cast out someone he is supposed to care for? Whatever the answer you may come up with, I wish someone would have told me an answer a long time ago.

The situation that would result in our being so hurt all started when I was a member at my dad's church where I played the drums. Things were going quite well in those days. I had my own drums that had been given to me when my mother purchased our first keyboard one Christmas. Soon after that purchase, I would add to my talents by learning to play the keyboard, and I even began to teach my younger brother to do the same. Later my brother and I began playing in my parents' church and quickly became the church musicians.

However, I constantly stayed in trouble, so my parents could not rely on me to be there for every service. They soon decided that they had to go on without me. They began giving my brother appreciation services, without ever mentioning my accomplishments at all. I felt as if they had forgotten about me, which led to my feeling rejected. After all, my musical abilities were an important aspect of my journey.

Far too often, we often assume that bad things are all bad for us, but God can "turn around" these bad happenings. Even though I was a troubled soul and never expected to receive such treatment, it was all for my good. I went into a depression and acted out my agony by reason of the pain I felt. I remember thinking, "I taught my brother everything I knew, and here he is getting all of the attention and praise." I watched this continue for quite some time until I was totally disconnected, had an "I-don't-care" attitude, and felt unappreciated.

One day I had an opportunity to play at a Baptist church where one of my friends attended. He knew I had talent and

Chapter 5: Cast Out, But Not Destroyed—Satan's Plot

constantly pursued me. So I complied and went to rehearsal with him. Apparently, the youth choir did not think favorably toward the older drummer who accompanied the youth choir. So my friend saw the perfect opportunity and suggested to them to give me a try.

Let's simply say that I was set up when he asked me to come to rehearsal. Anyway I was happy to oblige because I felt so rejected at my parents' church. Going to my friend's church was also my way of getting even with them. In truth, I was in heaven. There I was in an altogether different church without my parents and my brother, and I absolutely loved the freedom I felt. I mean, these people treated me like a king; I was suddenly now the "it" guy everyone wanted and appreciated. They gave me everything but money, and I didn't care; I was being cherished. I would travel with them from city to city and state to state as they performed. This church couldn't get enough of me, and I couldn't get enough of them. Being the center of attention was great.

Interestingly enough, I later discovered that the woman who played the organ had been praying for someone who was talented like me to show up. She apparently had a vision for the choir, and those involved didn't fit. So even though I had been rejected, someone was praying that I would show up—without even knowing my name. I learned a lesson that our God always has a plan, and though oftentimes it may seem bleak, He is still in control of our life. His purpose and plan for us always works in our favor, as it was now working for me. I needed a place to heal and lick my wounds, and the Lord guided me to a place where I could do exactly that.

The courtship by the church lasted for about three or four years, and my belonging was wonderful until one of the founding deacons of the choir died. Things began to change dramatically. He had been the heart and the soul of that choir; he was also the one who had kept us in order. Every person in that choir felt the pain of his loss and simply couldn't continue, and so we would soon part ways.

Many things happened after I left that ministry, but while I was still there, I was on a collision course with destiny. I would meet the man I was supposed to meet before I departed. When the time was right on an opportunistic day when we were scheduled to sing at another church, there he was. I did not know it at that time, but this mystery man would play a major role in my destiny. The time had come for me to move into the next level of my journey.

The Prophetic Moment

Knowing Christ is essential to a person's relationship to Him. If we say we know Him and do not keep His commandments, we have no part with Him. My flight was about to get very interesting as I would have to learn this truth. Before leaving the Baptist church, I met this man at another church one Sunday evening while playing drums for my choir. This man and his brothers had to croon at the same program and, as they say, they "stole the show"! They were really good.

After the service, this gentleman and I struck up a conversation after introducing ourselves. We only talked for a brief moment about my playing for them, how both of our parents were in the ministry, about music, and of all things, hair. Our topics of conversation sound funny, don't they! Well, he and I had a great deal in common. We both could sing, we both played more than one instrument, and we both had eccentric hair styles. I won't go into that fact; let it suffice to say that I was peculiar and different, and so was he!

He also shared with me that he was also a pastor and wanted me to visit his church. I told him that I would consider his invitation, so we exchanged numbers. Later while attending a service at my parents' church, this same man showed up there. I remember thinking, "What a coincidence!" or so I thought. I

Chapter 5: Cast Out, But Not Destroyed—Satan's Plot

now know I was on a collision with destiny.

Not long after the service ended, he approached me, but this time our conversation was quite different—anything but casual. He said, "I need to speak with you." He began prophesying, citing that God had a purpose for my life that was unknown to me. He added, "God said you are indeed called of God, and you are a minister." For me, that was the most I had ever heard God speak. His words were exactly what I needed after experiencing the rejection at my parents' church and after leaving the Baptist church.

In my mind after hearing this prophecy, I knew I would surely visit his church. Needless to say, when I got there, I stayed and became a member. I believed God willed me to be there; and I was exactly where He wanted me to be. I had obeyed the Lord; my destiny had now started. This was my prophetic moment.

I was now at a prophetic ministry, playing the drums and singing to the glory of God. I had landed in yet another place where I was greatly valued. Much to my surprise, I would later discover that my value was never about my talent.

Remember when I addressed the matter of obeying God in a previous chapter? Well, obeying God was relatively simple until the moment I began involving myself in this ministry. That's when I would be tested concerning keeping His commandments.

As time went on, I grew within the ministry because I was hearing the Word of God in such a way I had never before heard it preached. The pastor and I grew in friendship, and the church was growing at a rapid pace. We were always busy having musicals, inviting other speakers, hosting revivals and plenty of deliverance services. We also traveled on occasion to places like New York and Alabama, and sometimes I was privileged to go with my pastor. Yes, life was awesome.

What Lies Beneath?

Years passed, and everything was seemingly great until I started to notice certain patterns emerging within the ministry. This church had family issues—serious and involved issues that would eventually expel us from the ministry. Do you recall when I met this man, that he told me that his parents were in ministry? Well, not only were they in ministry, they were in the ministry under their son—the pastor! At first, things were going so well that I never stopped to see what might be lurking underneath the surface—until one day when the pastor's brother, who was the minister of music, quit! I soon discovered that their family was like my family, and the brothers were like my brothers, which makes the entire experience so bizarre.

Anyway, I was so shocked when the minister of music simply quit. Up until that point, I had never seen anyone quit in ministry. Shortly after he left, the pastor asked me to assume the role of minister of music and asked me to write him a detailed proposal specifying my future plans. I told him that I had already begun doing so, and that it would be completed soon.

When I was finished with my proposal, I gave it to him to read. He told me that the proposed plan was awe-inspiring. Consequently, he gave me the green light, and I quickly began to get things rolling again. Because I had my own way of doing things, the atmosphere became ugly—real ugly.

I was connected and had people I could call on to help with the music ministry, so I reached out to them. I enlisted the services of another keyboardist and a drummer, who I soon found had a mind of his own. On top of these issues, the following problems were cropping up:

- Rehearsals were great, but they were now structured—something they weren't used to seeing, and that was a problem.
- They didn't like the people I brought in to help. The fact that they were professionals was a problem.
- Some felt that it was taking too long for the choir to sing in a service. They did not like the time frame I set to debut the

Chapter 5: Cast Out, But Not Destroyed—Satan's Plot

choir, and that created another problem.
- The pastor's mother, whom I occasionally addressed as "Mother," was very jealous and protective of her son who had left the choir. Consequently, she did not like the fact he was no longer in charge. That was indeed a problem.
- The pastor's mother also felt because her other son was a pastor, she had the right to do and say anything she could think of. Believe me, that was a serious problem.

There I was in a strait between two places—whether to allow this insubordination, or try to ignore their murmuring, or replace these people and risk dealing with the ire of the pastor's mother and thereby jeopardize my friendship with the pastor. I was truly facing a tough decision, and the outcome either way was bad.

A Ministering Moment

I will not make any mention of the patterns I observed concerning their family; instead, I would like to draw attention to a controversial subject matter. A great number of pastors and church members won't like me for addressing this subject, but here goes anyway.

I was at a critical stage in ministry and I had befriended a pastor who had befriended me. However, I was a little too close to the man rather than Christ Jesus. The pastor was the ministry to me. I came to a point where I would tell him too much about my personal life. I even allowed him to make personal decisions pertaining to me, which ultimately led me to my first failed marriage.

I served him hand and foot, and I was happy doing so. I ran errands for him, I held his Bible, I wiped his sweat while he preached, and I even drove his car. The list of how I served this man goes on and on. Many did not like our closeness, and neither was his family in favor of our friendship.

> "Too often we in the church today lose ourselves in man and never find Christ."—Kevin L. Lipsey, Sr.

We sometimes serve these men as though they are kings, yet there is only one true King, and His name is Jesus! He's the King of kings and Lord of lords, end of story. We somehow place these pastors, as I did, upon a very high pedestal. If we don't somehow appease these men in some way, many of these pastors become offended.

The Word of God says in Matthew 23:11, "The greatest among you must be a servant." NLT

Jesus was the Master Teacher, yet He came to serve—not to be served. If you are going to serve someone, it must be Christ. The Word also talks about having no other god, but the one true living God before Him. We sometimes make men our gods, and they cannot compare. On assignment from God, they are as fallible as the next man. Please do not misunderstand me. I am not bashing pastors; I am simply trying to put things in prospective. We can serve God by serving others, but the excessiveness is much like a servant enslaved to a man rather than being a servant (a free moral agent) of Christ.

The Conclusion of What Lies Beneath

Now that I have shared this ministering moment, I must now address the tough, yet important side of this story. Subsequently, the pastor's mother and I had an argument one night, which led me to do the unthinkable. I was forced to put her in her place as a choir member. Of course, she immediately did what I thought she would do, she played the son card and went straight to her pastor-son. She had me called to the pastor's office, knowing good and well she was the one in the wrong. However, she had motives I did not see at the time, but were later revealed.

To make a long story short, he said what he said, she said what she said, and I said what I said. And the camaraderie

Chapter 5: Cast Out, But Not Destroyed—Satan's Plot

we shared was over—never to be the same again. As you can imagine, the plot only thickened. I was immediately on the radar as word quickly began spreading throughout the small, but big, family church. What happened after that was truly a test of my obedience to God. You see, I was on my way with the Lord (God was taking me somewhere), but I did not know it.

God had allowed me to go through this test in which the result would later be revealed in life—after even more test and trials. Little did I know that shortly after I met this pastor, I was being activated as a proponent of correction. Under the circumstances, I felt I was doing quite well outwardly, when inwardly I was going crazy.

The pastor called me to his house and said that he had something about which he wanted to talk to me. I felt okay because the following day, I was to debut the choir, so I had no reason to think anything negative was coming down. However, I had no way of knowing what was waiting for me. When I entered his house, I quickly discerned something was wrong—bad wrong. When I entered my pastor's house, he asked me to have a seat.

My heart began racing as my blood pumped like hot oil in a powerful V-8 engine. Suddenly, I was truly nervous! He began going through a long spiel about how God had a great purpose for me and that I had done an excellent job with the choir and music department. He said, "You are great for this ministry, and I wanted you—there no matter what…" But then he dropped a much unexpected bombshell. "But my brother wants to come back and assume his position, and I feel that I should let him." I could not believe what I was hearing; he was taking me down. The plotting of the mother was revealed.

I could not believe that the night before I was going to début the choir, I was being replaced by the guy who had abandoned them. I felt betrayed and rejected again as "patterns" had once again found me. I swallowed my pride and continued on.

The next day I sat in the pulpit and watched his brother direct the choir into which I had put my blood, sweat and tears. I couldn't look to the left or to the right; I felt as if all eyes were on me. Those watching couldn't believe what was happening, I had been effectively cast out.

The Consolation Prize

The choir sang beautifully, the musicians played skillfully, and the church was wonderfully blessed by the music program I had worked to achieve. After the service, many came to me and saluted me on a job well done; I guess they had figured it out. They obviously felt my pain and took sides immediately, but I wasn't having their pity. Hastily, I gave praise to the Lord and moved them toward the director to show them that in spite of the decision the pastor had made, we were presenting a united front. This was the correction God was showing them, but they never "got" it.

Before you begin thinking I was noble, let me share what happened during the offering before the service concluded. Right after the choir finished, the drummer whom I had brought in who had a mind of his own asked to meet me. Well, much to my surprise, he was an undercover prophet in training. He had apparently surmised my pain and frustration while playing the drums and was a witness to what went on. When he got off the drums, he made eye contact with me and asked me to step out of the pulpit and meet him in the back of the church where no one could see us. When we got there, he immediately fell to his knees and laid his hands on my feet.

What? I thought.

He said, "God told me to do this. You are one of God's generals!" He then prophesied that I had to endure these things because of where God was taking me. "The anointing on your life is great. Don't worry about this situation. Many other times will follow."

Chapter 5: Cast Out, But Not Destroyed—Satan's Plot

The drummer's words made me do what I did. Although I did not want what was happening to me, I could not stop it or what was to come. After all, "I was a marked man!" I had become a colossal threat against the powers of darkness, as well as to those who were willing to allow them room to operate.

More to Come

After this tough display of barely making it bravery, I felt torn and deeply wounded. I was like a badly beaten lion that after being overthrown in his kingdom, he left licking his wounds weak and alone. I was hurting bad. One of the most difficult things to do after such a traumatizing situation is to somehow continue on and forgive. I certainly was no exception to that rule. It's a sensitive place to be in after so much affliction and rejection.

Satan recognized my subsequent weakness and began eloquently laying traps and firing fiery dots ultimately designed to destroy me spiritually; thankfully, God was instituting something deeper—humility! This was now, "the now reality." I had to find a way to somehow cope with what had occurred, but I was finding coping very difficult. I wanted to leave the ministry and escape embarrassment, but as I stated, I knew this was the place where God had sent me.

So ultimately, because I had to, I decided to stay. I realized that if I were to stay the best thing I could do was to set boundaries. I felt if I simply did what God told me, like stay under the radar, and not get too involved, I could somehow escape the inevitable. What a farfetched concept in all of my spiritual reality! Simply put, "It wasn't going to happen!" How can I fly under the radar when God had obviously willed me to go through this heartbreak? I was now again on a collision course for destiny by way of adversity, pain and rejection. I was a recipient of what the Word of God called schisms in the body; and there was more to come.

"Trials come to make you strong and, in your weakness, He is made strong."

Scripture: "But the God of all grace, who hath called us unto his eternal glory by Christ Jesus, after that ye have suffered a while, make you perfect, establish, strengthen, settle you" (1 Peter 5:10).

Of course, I saw this truth as being anything but the truth. Nevertheless, within the course of time, I was proven wrong and God's Word prevailed.

Christ used division and refutation to draw me closer to him, while simultaneously correcting those with whom I would come in contact. Jesus Himself knew all too well about separation and rejection—being a spectacle while overcoming the world through it. Because I was in Christ, I too would be called to overcome; after all, there's no failure in Him so we can't fail. We who believe in Him are hidden in Him, but my response to it would determine my outcome.

Christ's response was that of love and forgiveness, and in exemplifying Him, we were called to do the same. Forgiving is easier said than done; however, it is not impossible. Even though we seemed to be failures, we found out that it's not how pretty you finish, but that you finish.

When this event occurred, I had not yet married Stephanie. Unbeknown to her, she too would have to endure trials and testing as a result of being married to me. Together, we would go through the fire—only to come out victoriously! The things we encountered together in ministry from this point on is truly a remarkable story, and we want to take you on our spiritual and emotional ride.

The Final Correction, Rejection, Ejection

If you're standing while reading this book, please sit. If you are lying down, please sit up. If you're doing more than one thing

Chapter 5: Cast Out, But Not Destroyed—Satan's Plot

while trying to read, stop. If you're thinking "This is not serious," think again. What I am about to say is in no way an attempt to implicate or to diminish anyone's character or reputation; rather, my goal is to reveal the true circumstances surrounding our growth in the Lord Jesus Christ.

Our goal is to expose Satan and his tactical failures in trying to consequently eradicate our work in the ministry, as well as his sincere efforts to try and destroy our relationship with God, and God's attempt to correct us.

Early one quiet Sunday morning around five o'clock a.m., the fallout began. My phone rang, and it was my pastor calling because he was about to leave town and wanted to give me some final instructions before his departure. By this time, Stephanie and I were married, and she had joined the church.

He told me that he had been called to preach at another church and that he was leaving me in charge to officiate the entire service. I complied and rolled over to get some more sleep before getting up to go to church that morning; after all, it was early. I got dressed, made sure my family was situated, and we left for church like every Sunday morning.

This Sunday was like any other day, with one exception: I was expected to carry out my pastor's wishes. I was to make sure that everything ran smoothly. Well, what was supposed to happen simply did not. When I came into the church building, I immediately went to the pastor's office where I was met with my first challenge. As soon as I entered the room, I discovered that some of the other ministers apparently did not receive Pastor's "memo." Two ministers on staff were busily planning their agenda. The others, including the pastor's brother, were conspicuously absent, but I found they had sent word that they were on the way.

One of them had told the two ministers already in the office not to start the service until he arrived and that he was officiating in the pastor's absence. The two ministers already in his office did not care for me; and knowing this, I carefully inserted that I had been personally contacted by Pastor and what he had conveyed to me what to do. I soon began to wonder, "Why did I do that?" as they proceeded to tell me something totally different than I had been told.

A Very Important Announcement

The people meeting with me in that office were some of the people within the church who did not care for me. I believe this meeting was a product of one of Satan's many attempts to create a schism and to try to force my wife and me to leave this ministry. Some were jealous of my friendship with the pastor, and the fallout between the pastor's mother and me caused division. Even though I knew how they felt, I never let them know I knew their true feelings concerning me.

I believe satanic forces were at an all-time high regarding this matter. He wanted me to abort the plan and purpose for my life by getting me to forfeit my ministry. Schisms are very dangerous within the body of Christ; they cause us to do horrible things to one another, thereby prohibiting a move of God. Of course, emotions like envy, strife, anger, malice and wrath show their ugly faces in this moment, causing serious damages, and sometimes irreparable harm to the body of Christ. Another quote from my message entitled "Acquainted with Grief" explains it as follows:

> Blessed ("be happy") when men revile you and persecute you. You who are persecuted for righteousness' sake, rejoice and be exceedingly glad because the very fact that you're going through persecution means God is saying that it is necessary for what He is about to release in your life!

Chapter 5: Cast Out, But Not Destroyed—Satan's Plot

The Conclusion

After explaining the matter to them, apparently my cries were ignored. In their own authority and against the pastor's wishes, they proceeded to override the instructions given to me. A spokesperson said, "We too have talked to the pastor, and he did not mention that he left you to administrate." They lied!

I couldn't believe what I was witnessing. Theirs was an all-out blatant act of insubordination within the sanctity of the church. But then, I couldn't help but think, as if that is a new ploy of Satan's.

So we prayed without the others, and I don't know how we could have agreed at that point, but I did it anyway and began the morning service. Shortly afterward, to make matters worse, after I had relented, like clockwork, the pastor's brother came in and began to take over the service—exactly like he said he would. "What is going on?" Truly, I was lost for words at what I was witnessing. The pastor's brother, who came in late after we had been waiting for quite some time, proceeded to interrupt the service which had already started, not only took control, but in the middle of praise and worship, he stopped the flow of the service to tell me that he wanted to read a Scripture! What?

I whispered to him that it wasn't the appropriate time to proceed with a Scripture, and that we would do it immediately after praise and worship had concluded. He vehemently disagreed with what I said, pursued his own suggestion, and swiftly executed his decision. While this interacting was going on, we were in front of the congregation, who could see the exchange. To make matters worse, the mother of my pastor and his brother, was sitting on the front row watching everything. She had a look of disgust on her face as she surmised that I was going against one of her sons. Someone else was also watching.

While I was trying to handle matters in a respectable manner, the pastor's brother continued to try to take over, so again I gave in because I did not want the church members to see this dissension. He obviously didn't care. I felt very sad that matters were heading in this direction, so I decided to step down and allow him to carry on. My wife and I retreated to the back of the sanctuary throughout the remainder of the service. Shortly before the service was over, their mother stood up to make an announcement that she wanted to have a meeting with all of the ministers, and then looking directly at me, she added, "and the so-called minister."

Like King Belshazzar, I saw the proverbial handwriting on the wall; I did not want any part of the meeting. Before I could get out of the front door, I was asked by someone if I was staying, and I said, "No!" I quickly hurried to my car, and as I was pulling out of the parking lot, the pastor's brother knocked on my window. "Are you staying for the meeting?"

Again I replied, "No!"

On our way home, my wife asked, "Why didn't you stay?"

I said, "I would have been like raw meat in a den of wolves. Their mother was after me, and I know she was because of her announcement."

Stephanie and I were in shock at their aggression toward me. I truly did not understand what was going on. Days passed as I was left to ponder and go over in my mind the chain of events that had transpired at the church. Stephanie and I went over the scenario multiple times; we simply could not come up with a viable answer for their vitriolic hostility. I toiled and toiled for days, eagerly awaiting my pastor's return so that he could straighten out this mess. Surely he could shed some light on the matter and vindicate me by telling his staff that he had indeed left me in charge.

How can an apparent moderate unassuming task go so terribly wrong so quickly? I had one assignment to do—make sure that everything ran smoothly. All I could think was that I had failed miserably, or did I?

I was totally unprepared for what was yet to come. I had

Chapter 5: Cast Out, But Not Destroyed—Satan's Plot

no clue as to what would befall me after I had declined to go to a meeting that the pastor's mother had no business calling. She had absolutely no authority to do so, but she had exercised what she thought she had the right to do anyway. She had an agenda, and I was on her hit list. I was not prepared for what her pastor-son would do, although I thought that he would surely understand and vindicate me.

The Untold Part

Before I continue with my narration, I must share that before all of this occurred and after the choir bit, a great deal of good had happened. Indeed, some things were bad, but a lot of things were very good. However, a few people within the ministry had it out for me, and their jealousy ran very deep.

The pastor had often stood for me in situations where my enemies thought that I should have been removed. Some people thought that I had somehow been receiving preferential treatment. I had no idea that some of these people actually despised me; I had thought that they were a little jealous, but to my surprise, their jealousy had turned to hatred and resentment. They felt I was moving too fast and that the pastor had placed too much confidence in me. Some, who even wanted my position, did not realize that promotion comes from God and that the Lord had instructed the pastor to prep me for the pastorate. This was the reason why he was doing so many things with me and why it appeared to many as if I was receiving special treatment. My pastor was simply heeding God's command to prepare me to one day have my own work. Nonetheless, these same people applied tremendous amounts of pressure to the pastor, and he eventually succumbed to their wishes. Indeed, this time was heavy—very heavy.

How could this happen—especially when this pastor knew of the mandate given to him by God for my benefit? How important is it for us to obey God? The waiting on God in this incident was that God's purpose for my life was to be fulfilled at this ministry; however, my pastor didn't wait.

The Word of God says in 1 Corinthians 4:5,

> "Therefore judge nothing before the time, until the Lord come, who both will bring to light the hidden things of darkness, and will make manifest the counsels of the hearts: and then shall every man have praise of God."

This was not the case with me, and you will see as I have previously stated how schisms can affect our lives within the body of Christ. The people judged the situation and eventually passed a ruling not in my favor. Did they wait for God to bring to light that hidden thing? Will I finally see their true motives by God's revealing their hearts? I knew I needed answers and soon. I needed my Master to help me because the weapon had now been formed. The question was, "Will that weapon prosper?"

The Season Finale

Please brace yourselves because nothing can possibly prepare you for the finale of my story. Although I have already shared the end of the matter, I want to explain what happened step by step.

A couple of days had passed since the incident; and by now, I was sure that the pastor had heard of it. After many attempts to reach him unsuccessfully, he finally called me, stating he wanted to meet with me. "How soon can you get to the church?" He made his request seem as though the meeting involved only the two of us. I wanted to give him a full and accurate account on the event, so I agreed to meet with him—even though I could discern that something was terribly wrong in his voice.

I drove to the church, nervously rehearsing what I planned to say, and not knowing what was really waiting for me once I arrived at the church. The closer I got to the church, the more

Chapter 5: Cast Out, But Not Destroyed—Satan's Plot

fretful I became until I finally arrived and saw that not only had I been called to the meeting, but all of those people who hated me were also there.

Apparently his family had quickly bombarded him with "facts" before he and I could make contact and talk. They obviously had ample time to plead their case to him without my being there to defend myself. As a result, some preconceived judging had already followed. I felt I was about to be another castaway; however, not one on Gilligan's Island, but more like one on the "isle of Patmos." Yes, if the apostle John had still been alive, he would have had some company—and not the Holy Ghost. After eluding the wolves for the first meeting, I had once again been invited to "dinner," and this time, I was going to be served.

Chow Time

I walked into this meeting, and I recognize right away that I had no chance of making it out of there alive. The meeting began with the pastor's asking me a question to which he already knew the answer. You probably remember the type of question from when you were a kid. His question was the kind parents ask their children. "Didn't I tell you not to touch that?" You simply know you are about to get blasted, and get blasted bad.

He fired questions at me: "What happened? Why didn't you listen to my mother? Why did you leave when she asked you to stay for the meeting?"

I was being accused as if he already knew I was guilty. Nothing I had said in the car to prepare myself registered. I simply could not think of anything to say in my defense. I understood what was happening, and my mind registered the cleverness of the Enemy's strategy; I was rightfully angered. The pastor conveniently noticed, and another minister in the meeting started citing accusations. "He came to church that Sunday morning, trying to take over—as if he had been put in charge."

"Sure," I thought, "that is true, seeing as how the pastor

called my house earlier that morning to corroborate this claim."

He then stated that I was uncooperative and demanding. "When I did not get my way, I just shut down."

At this point, I was looking for my pastor to shut down the meeting. I thought he had the perfect opportunity to tell everyone present that he did, in fact, leave me in charge. What I was looking for flat out never happened! He never told anyone there that he had indeed called me or had said anything to me!

So I called him out on it, and he flat out denied that such a conversation had ever taken place! In other words, he lied.

I could not believe all of the accusations; one after another, the claims kept coming. Both of the pastor's brothers, who had been like brothers to me, stuck together telling lie after lie. The one who came in late was the obvious ring leader, and the other one who had left the choir started spewing like a baby who had just been burped. He even started bringing up my past and making comments like: "You hurt me." He even threw in my face how much they had helped me in the past. The other cited that I was somehow being insubordinate. Then he challenged my salvation because I had asked him not to read a Scripture. He conveniently forgot to mention that praise and worship was in full swing; and that the presence of the Lord was there—well, at least until he arrived. "Smiley face!"

Shortly afterward, the woman minister who was in the office when I arrived that Sunday decided to get in on the action too. I can testify that she went into areas that caught everyone in the room off guard. She started making ridiculous statements like how she hated me because I was now divorced from my ex-wife, who happened to be her friend. "He shouldn't be allowed in ministry," she boldly stated. I will never forget how she sat right next to me and told everyone there she absolutely "hated" me. Wow!

All I can say is that I was floored. I was eaten alive while the people biting and devouring me were getting full and belch-

Chapter 5: Cast Out, But Not Destroyed—Satan's Plot

ing all the things they hated about me to my face. I felt like I was in a venting and eating session. Soon they all began bringing up my past, mentioning personal things I confided in private and trusted to them in confidence. They trampled my act of what I had thought was obedience to God and to my pastor's wishes. I found neither comfort nor friend in the room that awful night.

The drummer I hired—the young man who prayed for me when the choir debuted—was also present, and from the beginning he had an agenda to stay neutral. When it seemed like someone should have come to my rescue, to me this person was it, but he was worse than anyone in the room. Why you ask? He was neither hot nor cold. "We all know what the scripture says about that!" Nevertheless, when the pastor noticed that he wasn't saying anything, he asked him for his opinion on the matter. You know, he asked, "What do you think about this situation?"

Remember! This young man had met me in the back of the sanctuary to encourage me by giving me a word from the Lord. He was the drummer who had a mind of his own. He was a supposed friend who apparently loved the pastor and his family as much as I did; however, his relationship to me evidently wasn't as valuable as his relationship to the pastor. It no longer seemed to matter to him that I was the one who had brought him to the ministry. Sure we had some common interests, and were fairly close in friendship—but he would often do strange things like butter up to the pastor and his family to gain favor. Nevertheless, what followed was more like something out of a movie than a church ministry, and would prove to be our demise.

So the pastor asked him how he felt; however, since his loyalty to both parties caused him to remain neutral, the pastor got clever and decided to give him an ultimatum, thereby forcing him to choose sides. When he couldn't or wouldn't choose, he told us that we both had to leave. I was being cast out of ministry and didn't understand. On the other hand, I was far too crushed to even think about it. Moving on!

Feels Like Another One

I am told that time heals all wounds, but I am inclined to think that it's more about licking the wounds and taking care of them before time expires and something worse happens. There is something about adding on and making things more terrible, and though the last ministry didn't heed God's correction, I was still being used as Paul would say—"a fool for Christ sake." By this time, I was well into on-the-job training. Nevertheless, one thing was evidently clear; we became stronger in the power of God's might, and if we were going to make it through, we had to trust in Him.

This was the case with my wife and me at this point in our lives. God had us on the fast track as proponents of correction, and we only had a limited amount of time before arriving at the next ministry. So we had to suck it up, tend to our wounds, and quickly move on because more was yet to come. We needed to be prepared.

By this time I'd experienced so much hurt and pain in ministry, that deep down I really desired a spiritual father. I needed to face facts. My previous life had displayed a series of complex patterns that had dictated my life. Now I was at the point where I had had enough; I knew I needed a spiritual father. Both my biological father and my stepfather had betrayed me and now my former pastor had joined their ranks. This time I needed someone on whom I could rely.

I needed someone who could understand me. I needed someone patient and wise and someone who could guide me through life's many obstacles while teaching me the things of God and watching over my soul. This very real emotion led us to the next ministry where I would soon find that God had a plan; and that our learning was far from being over.

We touched down in this meticulous ministry (which shall remain anonymous) by way of an old family friend who

Chapter 5: Cast Out, But Not Destroyed—Satan's Plot

in times past was my babysitter. In fact, this was so particular, I couldn't recall a single solitary truth my wife and I learned with the exception of two things: how not to be in ministry and the opposite of that which is order. This pastor, in my view, was paranoid, but orderly; detailed, yet edgy; intelligent, yet fragile. This kind of ministry was very new to us at the time and, in spite of the complexity of the situation, we were determined to go on and see what the end was going to be.

Who Are You Really?

Upon our arrival to this ministry, the pastor and I hit it off pretty well. It seemed as though whatever church we went to, I knew some people there. Such was the case as I approached the pastor and the ministry. I saw an old familiar face I had befriended years prior, and he conveyed to the pastor who I was. They quickly focused on my talents and worth to the ministry.

I must say that my talents were/and are great; I wouldn't take anything for them, but sometimes you simply want people to see you—not your gifts or talents. Seemingly, everywhere I went, I was being exploited for what I could do. I had never received any interest for me, but this was all about to change with a chance prophetical meeting with a woman whom I had never before seen until that moment.

Before I share what happened, I must say that this next ministry was very intimidating and excellent at the same time. The people did everything right; they were so orderly and nice to everyone—but almost like robots programmed to do definite tasks.

Anyway, right away the pastor wanted me next to him, which I thought was quite strange—seeing how I had just gotten there. I would see this strange phenomenon again and again as every ministry I went to, the pastor would discern my anointing, having never even met me. I felt like I had become his right-hand man. I would help him accomplish many things as I worked in the church office on a daily basis. I felt like I had walked through the front door and went straight to work. I quickly adjusted and felt reassured by quite a change of scenery after experiencing the letdown of a lifetime at my previous ministry.

I even helped him on a few exams while he was in college/seminary. Yes, I decided, "This is the place for my family and me." All was well with thee, or so I thought.

Remember my belief that this pastor was paranoid? When I arrived one day, he called me to have a meeting with him. In that meeting he asked me about my previous ministry, and I shared some of the unpleasant things that had happened to us without implicating my former pastor. He even asked if I wanted to go back and would ask quite often, "What's up with that?"

He did not believe me nor could he see my pain or me as a person. So he did the unthinkable and contacted my former pastor to request a meeting—all while conveniently forgetting to mention his intention to me.

By this time, I was working at the ministry, which again happened very quickly. As I was walking out of the sanctuary into the foyer area of the church, approaching the hallway to the pastor's office, imagine who I ran into? You guessed correctly! My former pastor was walking through the door! He walked toward me, looked me square in the eye, and passed me without saying one word. I was shocked. I felt an enormous amount of pain and betrayal, rehashing everything that had happened. I felt like someone had reopened my healing wounds and poured salt on them again.

Well, as you might well envision, I could not stay to imagine the possible outcome of such a conference, so I left, contemplating the dreadful outcome. I was confused and hurt, asking myself, why is he here? Why did my current pastor do this to me? Why? I was once again in a situation that was so familiar to me.

One thing led to another after that meeting. The first inkling my wife and I had was to abruptly leave the ministry; how-

Chapter 5: Cast Out, But Not Destroyed—Satan's Plot

ever, as I have already stated, my God had a plan. That plan was being laid out before me, but I simply couldn't see it.

If He brought me out of the last one, surely He would prove Himself powerful yet again.

The pastor did not immediately speak to me of the meeting; in fact, I had to ask him about the final results. Would you have ever expected that he would want to keep their meeting confidential? What in the world? He had a meeting with my former pastor about me, and he was treating the information as privileged? What was that all about? I discovered he wanted to use his newfound information in order to justify his not advancing me in the ministry!

A Ministering Moment

Do you know the story of Joseph in the Bible? So many wonderful things can be said about Joseph's life; however, let me draw your attention to his telling his brothers of the dream which he had. To me, what is significantly obvious is what follows: his being cast out, or should I say, cast in and left for dead. Here's what I'm saying, my friend. Sometimes we can make statements with little knowledge or understanding of its possible repercussion. We are purely and honestly oblivious to its tumultuous effects.

Such was the case with Joseph, and such was the case with me. I had prematurely spoken of some matters with my pastor, and obviously, he wasn't ready to receive them—like Joseph's brothers. Consequently, like Joseph, I was cast in a spiritual dungeon—left to figure out, "What just happened?"

Joseph's jealous brothers had the upper hand or so they thought; the real story focused on Joseph, his spiritual growth, and his purpose. God had a plan for me, and while I was in my "dungeon," He finally spoke to me. If I really did not know who I was or if it wasn't clear to me as well as others, it was about to come out.

I Didn't See It Coming

My current pastor would ask me to perform several menial tasks, only stating that he wanted to see "If you are humble…" Because of my commitment to the Lord, I complied with his requests. He had me doing everything from cleaning the bathrooms to parking cars in the parking lot—all while constantly asking for my help and advice on his personal school exams.

As I think of these times, I am reminded of the Scripture in Deuteronomy 18:21, which refers to knowing whether or not a prophet was speaking truth to you. I must admit that I did not know if what he had me doing was God authorized; nevertheless, I did according to the Word by asking God if the sometimes absurd requests my pastor asked of me was Him or about my pastor's knowing who I was before I did. Many questions crossed my mind constantly. What did this man discern about me? What was he so afraid of? More importantly, what was I projecting? From the beginning while working with him, he would always ask me how I knew what I knew, and I would always respond by giving God the glory.

Yes, he was intelligent, but he had no real experience with God. So he marveled at the anointing given to me by God, which caused unwarranted jealousy. Not only did he never intend to advance me, but he kept me close to him, sucking me dry for information from God (my anointing) and would often use what God had given me in his messages. Yes, I was being used as a means to a private end.

But as I ponder on the story of Joseph, I have realized that his brothers feared what he was to become; so instead of helping him, they did everything they could to impede his dream from coming to pass. This pastor knew of this concerning me and inevitably pursued the same path, but what God had for me was greater than anyone could hamper.

One day my wife and I had a brief meeting with the pastor following the morning service. I cannot recall anything un-

Chapter 5: Cast Out, But Not Destroyed—Satan's Plot

usual with the exception of what followed. As the pastor, my wife and I were walking out of the sanctuary, a couple—a beautiful elderly woman with silky, black-and-gray hair and her husband—walked right in my path and stopped in front of me.

I was standing there thinking, What in the world is going on? Who is this woman? Why is she standing here staring at me? She simply stood in front of me gazing into my eyes for several seconds. Then she proceeded to prophesy to me before God, my wife, and the pastor. She said, "Hi, bishop!"

The pastor assumed she was referring to him, but he knew as well as my wife and me to who she was referring. Of course, I hesitated for a brief moment, and finally I responded and said,

"Who me?"

"Yes!" she said, "I'm talking to you. God has called you a bishop, and I see it all over you." She then repeated, "You are a bishop." With those words, she and her husband simply walked away, leaving my wife, the pastor, and me to ponder what had taken place.

I often find it peculiar how our God chooses to do His work; yet, He's so on time. I simply asked the Lord to reveal to me His purpose for my life, and here He was encouraging me through this lady. I never saw it coming!

Yes, God had previously revealed to me through the drummer at my former ministry, but never had I ever been called a bishop! Prophecy was being fulfilled right before my eyes; the drummer had spoken it, so if he got this right, I knew I was in for more.

Again, do not forget this book addresses the importance of waiting on God. My Heavenly Father was ultimately causing me to be joined with His purpose and intent for my life, and He wasn't about to stop for the roadblocks I was experiencing. So my wife and I celebrated this small victory on the road to Damascus. I was in a better place spiritually, and I could now labor on and see the end result of His plans.

Many wonderful things happened at that ministry, and I was glad to be a part of it. However, shortly after a few other instances of the pastor's controlling ways, we parted ways after hearing clearly from the Lord. "Why?" In truth, the pastor couldn't take it anymore. Jealousy enraged him, and because of his calculating ways, when my wife and I missed a couple of services, he assumed that I was either looking for another ministry or courting my former pastor. He simply called my house and told me that we were no longer welcome at that ministry.

Sure, the result is a seemingly unfortunate occurrence; but as I have already addressed, if the affliction meant promotion, then certainly Stephanie and I were in for a serious blessing. However, more training was needed before that could happen. From our viewpoint, we were simply hoping that the promotion from God was upon us.

Moving Forward

Slightly wounded and despondent from the experience of two pastors turning against us and with very little progressive faith from which to glean, my wife and I unenthusiastically moved in pursuit of our next stop on this God journey. We had a great deal to process. To us, it was beginning to look like every church we stepped foot in was a proponent of correction God used to teach us more of Him. We were also beginning to feel like church hoppers, and I certainly am not an advocate of what is known as "church hopping." I realized that something peculiar was happening over which I had little to no control. My wife and I simply felt compelled to go with the flow of what God was doing.

It's a mind-augmenting reality when we are suddenly confronted with the truth of God in some of the most unlikely places. When a rare opportunity presents itself, we must embrace it with all grace and humility, while bracing ourselves for what will surely be revealed. This happened to me one day while endeavoring to work around my home; the continuation of such

Chapter 5: Cast Out, But Not Destroyed—Satan's Plot

came upon me, and the conclusion to the matter of truth came.

While it is true that Jesus claims to be "the Truth," we fail to realize that this certainty is revealed to us perpetually. The Scripture declares that we are to be forever learning, and yet we can never fully come into the knowledge of the truth. God ordained this to be so for many obvious reasons, one is which of pride.

- Pride is primarily the absence of God in a person's conscience. You know, the proud person willingly and decisively says, "I know it all"! The haughty spirit comes before a fall because we feel that the partial truth that God has given us is the whole. Simply stated, the proud person is not interested in obtaining the sum total of truth.
- Two, God never gives us the fullness until we have been proven to be worthy. Only the Heavenly Father is capable of managing such a thing. Even then we have not yet arrived at this juncture. Purely on the basis of the vastness of the God Whom we serve, an eternity will be required to begin to know His fullness and then some.
- Three, learning is continual. Once a truth in part is revealed by God, it has to be tested, not only by other so-called truths, but by God's truth. "Why?" Well, being that our God is just, and in recalling a little matter called free moral agency, while revealing a truth given in part, He proves the truth by simultaneously making a show of others through our free choice. We then, by "His Spirit," are presented with an option thereby to see the obvious (that God is good) and to lay hold of God's Truth and denounce falseness. It took me some time to gather pieces of God's truth, joining them together to see a picture forming before my eyes; His truth reveals and illuminates.

This action grows us and yet brings us to an ultimate reality; we must continue to rely on God and never stop learning of Him through His Word (the Truth).

> "Because we only know in part, we should never feel as though we have arrived when we only have been given partial lessons."—Kevin L. Lipsey, Sr.

Let us continue to grow in the grace of God with humility and refinement. A revealed truth about our God is but a fraction of His person, His love, His majesty, His omnipotence, His omnipresence, His omniscience, His Excellency and all that He is.

Never stop learning of Him and the things pertaining to this life. With persistence and patience, we will one day behold the Truth. These mortal bodies will never be able to contain all there is to know of Him, only to things pertaining to life on earth and what He chooses to reveal. This revelation of knowledge is based on our willingness to seek after God.

The Word of God declares:

"O the depth of the riches both of the wisdom and the knowledge of God! How unsearchable are his judgments, and his ways past finding out. For who hath knowledge of the mind of the Lord? Or who hath been his counselor? Or who hath first given to him, and it shall be recompensed unto him again? For of him, and through him, and to him, are all things: to whom be glory forever. Amen" (Romans 11:33-36; KJV).

After this brief happening, my wife and I would get on board with yet another one of God's lessons. God annulled everything that He couldn't use; He stripped us of all or what little "pride" we had left. There is a tremendous price to pay for truth in Christ; however, neither Stephanie nor I for that matter, had

Chapter 5: Cast Out, But Not Destroyed—Satan's Plot

the ability or the means to pay this price. We would meekly have to rely on God to forgive us of this debt we owed Him by continually surrendering our lives to Him. Thus, we permitted Him to finish the work He began in us. We had come so far, and He was completing the work. We knew this purging was required of us as stewards, and that as ministers, we would be found faithful.

WAITING ON GOD

Chapter 6:
God's Boot-Camp

THE BIBLE SAYS IN PROVERBS 16:18 THAT "PRIDE GOETH before destruction, and an haughty spirit before a fall." As I thought about this verse, I also thought that surely I was not guilty of pride…at least I'd like to think so. I know we had encountered a great deal along the way, but pride and me? No way—not me! This is what I kept hearing during a brief period before arriving at our next destination. If any pride was left in me or in my wife after what we had already been through, God was about to extract it in a big way.

The pride extraction process all started when my wife and I left our previous ministry and felt a massive appetite for the truth in Christ. We had to believe that there was more to knowing God than our encountering non-loving Christians while on our road to Damascus. There had to have been a reason for our enduring so much pain and agony, but we simply couldn't figure it out. By this time we had preconceived notions as to how and what we wanted, over which neither of us had any control, but no one could have told us that. One thing was for certain: I was finished with the whole "father" in the ministry deal.

A Divine Appointment

We needed answers before going to the next place, and we needed them fast. Our appetite for truth grew stronger and stronger; we desired spiritual food, and the grace of God supplied! While working at the salon one day, my wife encountered a rather peculiar client who happened to be a bishop. That day he had handlers with him because of his advanced age and some minor health issues he had developed. One of the handlers explained to my wife that he was looking for someone to maintain his hair, and that if she did a great job to his liking, she would gain a new customer.

Needless to say, my wife pleased him, and in the process, we gained a friend. After a few hair shampoos and trims, my wife told the bishop in a conversation that I was a minister. That brief exchange compelled him to want to meet me.

When I met Bishop Rice, I immediately knew that he was a man sent from God by divine appointment. He spoke of Christ with such eloquence and grace, yet with power and confidence—in a manner I had never before heard. We were intrigued and drawn to this great mystery of Christ being revealed to us. After being reared in church all of our lives, Christ had now come to us. I felt as if He had physically come into the room to allow us to touch Him, to take hold of Him, to know Him, and so we did.

Bishop Rice grew to love us, and he began treating me as a son in the ministry. He even offered me the pastorate of one of his twenty-six churches after hearing what we had experienced, but I knew he wasn't to be the father for whom I had been searching. The bishop later confirmed these thoughts by telling me the following: "God says to stop searching for a father because He (God) is your Father."

Before ever seeing Bishop Rice again, we were invited to his pastoral anniversary and witnessed this seventy-two-year-old man of God preach Christ for five straight hours one final time. He had recently suffered a heart attack! I am not exaggerating! My wife and I got the message: it was all about Jesus…and no

Chapter 6: God's Boot Camp

one else! God wanted us to know Christ, and He used Bishop Rice to re-introduce Him to us. We were already Christian believers, but the revelation of Christ was illuminated to us on a greater level. We were never the same. Thank you, Bishop Rice!

The Guy on the Radio

One sunny afternoon while riding in our car we were listening to AM talk radio. Stephanie and I tuned in to a preacher whose name I knew from previous years. Though I did not know him formally, I knew of him. His son and daughter knew my brother very well. Apparently, my older brother and his daughter dated briefly, and her brother and my brother played basketball together. Even so, I ultimately visited their church on occasion for totally different reasons.

In my city in previous years, church musicals were very popular. I was a part of those tuneful sessions as a singer, songwriter or producer. When I was in my early twenties, I began dating a young lady who was affiliated with a well-known choir I'd worked with on occasion. This particular preacher and his church were known to host these events frequently, and my then girlfriend's choir would sing there. They harbored some of the best singers known at that time!

As we were listening to the radio, we began noticing this particular preacher/teacher (could make a strong case for "truth crusader") was expounding on the Word of God in a manner which we had never before heard—except through our friend, Bishop Rice. His exegesis of Scripture was so overwhelmingly breathtaking that we began tuning in every day. We both felt refreshed to hear "the word" in truth and without all the extra drama. He revealed Christ in an incredible way, by conjoining the Old Testament with the New Testament, conveying how Christ was always there. Just like that, his messages clicked with us.

No words could really explain how we felt after hearing this preacher for several days on his talk radio show. He spoke of subjects and defined them in ways I had never before heard, such as:

- Apologetics
- Systematic theology
- World religions
- Atheism (Atheists are people who believe that god or gods are manmade constructions.)
- Baha'i (one of the newest world major religions)
- Buddhism (a way of living based on the teachings of Siddhartha Gautama)
- Christianity (the world's biggest faith based on the teaching of Jesus Christ)
- Hinduism (a group of faiths rooted in the religious ideas of India)
- Islam (revealed in its final form by the prophet Muhammad)
- Jehovah's Witnesses (A supposed Christian-based evangelistic religious movement)
- Judaism (based around the Jewish people's covenant relationship with God)
- Mormonism (the Church of Jesus Christ of Latter-day Saints)
- Paganism (contemporary religions usually based on reverence for nature)
- Spiritualism (a religion believing in communication with the spirits of deceased people)
- Unitarianism (an open-minded and individualistic approach to religion)

He spoke of people, including:

- Francis Schaeffer, a great American evangelical theologian, philosopher
- Norman L. Geisler, a Christian apologist and the co-founder of the Southern Evangelical Seminary

Chapter 6: God's Boot Camp

- Dr. Ron Rhodes, a popular author, conference speaker, and seminar leader who founded and presides over "Reasoning from the Scriptures," a ministry dedicated to training and educating Christians in the Word of God and in apologetics
- Ni To-sheng, who is better known as Watchman Nee, served as a church leader and Christian teacher in China during the first half of the twentieth century.
- Hank Hanegraaff, president and chairman of the board of the Christian Research Institute International.

Finally! Finally, I had found someone to whom I could relate in Christ and grow from. Sure he spoke of things I had no way of knowing, but I felt as though God was speaking directly to me through this man. Stephanie felt the same way. In our minds we wanted to meet this man face to face, so we pursued! Finally, We Meet!

At this moment in time and space I'm feeling a little happy, because it's a particular Sunday and my wife and I finally decided to visit the pastor's church after listening to him on the radio. Finally, I would meet "the truth crusader." When we arrived, at first we were somewhat nervous, and that nervousness was quickly elevated even more with what happened when we walked in.

Remember? "Waiting on God" entails our being joined together to meet the complete purpose that God has for our life—to lie in wait for someone!

Well, as soon as we walked into the church, this pastor to whom we had been listening on the radio, suddenly called to me, saying: "You sir; you, yes you! Come up here with me, I need you up here with me."

I was completely dumbfounded by his order! Even though I shouldn't have thought it strange, I did. If you are a Bible scholar, you know what I'm talking about (1 Peter 4:12).

My wife and I were shocked. We were both wondering,

"What just happened?" This man did not know me and I did not know him, but he had just called me up to sit with him on the side of the pulpit where he and the other ministers sat. He said to me, "When I saw you, God told me to call you to the front with me because that is where you belong." He also said that I was to stay by him, and that I was to come to church for Wednesday night Bible study where he would announce me to the entire church.

My mind was whirling. "What in the world is happening?!" Talk about an awesome experience; this was "over the top." I finally could envision life going right for my family and me. However, even though God had told me not to look for a father, I still had issues with the entire "father figure in the ministry." I was looking for validation. I desired for God to prove to people that He was with me, and that proof would put an end to all this warfare we were encountering. Nevertheless, I simply did not understand that "the going through" was the validation needed to accomplish the ministry in which we would partake in the future.

Wednesday Night

You can imagine how I was feeling and what I was thinking after sitting in a service with the preacher to whom I had been listening on the radio? Not only that, when he had seen me the very first time, he had called me to the front of the church to sit with him, telling me that God had told him to do so. What was I thinking? Well, I was in church, but then again, I wasn't! You can imagine how the conversation on the way home went with Stephanie, and how our talk and wonder continued until Wednesday night's service.

I honestly didn't know what to expect. What would he say to me? What would he say to the church? Why was God choosing this church for my wife and me?

We went to the service on Wednesday, and an eternity

Chapter 6: God's Boot Camp

seemed to pass as we waited for this man to do what he said God had told him to do. Right before the benediction, the pastor began to share with the congregation in a different fashion what he had told me three days earlier.

"Ladies and gentleman, do you see this young man? God sent him here for you and for me. I don't know to what extent, however, all I can tell you is that God sent him here! You are to respect him as you would me because God sent him here…"

Just like that, I was suddenly right next to this pastor. He even had me speak on his radio show! Once again, God had found a way to put me next to the pastor—as I had miraculously been at the previous ministry. You are probably thinking, "This routine sounds familiar." I can promise that this opportunity felt different—to what extent, I did not have a clue. We began to pray.

If ever there was a story with the feel of Alice in Wonderland with me in it as key character, I was living it—I was Alex in Wonderland. I felt that my wife and I were finally in a place where we could grow in the grace of God, and we were surrounded by people who were full of the Spirit of God.

We could fellowship with one another in love; the preaching/teaching, and the music was absolutely impeccable. We were completely satisfied with God's choice, and in our minds, it simply could not get any better than what we had encountered.

A Ministering Moment

I once heard a preacher teaching on the subject of "Opportunity," who mentioned that opportunity comes in three forms:

1. Problems. The bigger the problem, the greater the potential of blessing that is perhaps coming your way.
2. Crisis. A divine announcement that God wants to move you to the next level of blessing and promotion.
3. Rejection. We simply must change our view amid refusal or

denials, which serves to redirect our focus while engaging us in an insightful experience.

Waiting on God is also recognizing His voice when He speaks; the level of training in this field is accomplished through trial and error (problems) on our part coupled with God's ability to suffer long with us as a Father as we will make mistakes! However, God's longsuffering can be multi-dimensional as well as multifarious.

Waiting on God affords us with an opportunity to be tried and tested through God-designed rejections. This action breeds an extensive prayer life, which is needed in the difficult intervals of life. During these critical periods, God will speak with exactitude and accuracy; however, we must be mature enough to discern and hear His voice.

The author Ron Rhodes explains it like this:

> Scripture is clear that the Holy Spirit is to illuminate the minds of Christians, so that we can understand not only the voice of God, but also how He works. His transmitting is a perfect signal; however, it is we whose radio dials need adjusting!

This is where the problem or crisis usually enters. We're the ones who are in need of an adjustment to reach the next level. God did this with the Apostle Paul while he was in prison—his problem/his crisis.

> "God will deliver us to the blessing, while elevating our understanding of Him through problems He intends to solve..."—Kevin Lipsey, Sr.

It's not about the problem, it's about the adjustment (or lesson) in the problem.

Chapter 6: God's Boot Camp

They Didn't Like It

If I was about to receive a blessing, then may I simply skip the massive problem that arose? I mean, certainly God through His omnipotence, can decide to do so without anyone's questioning His authority, right? At least I have learned that you have to go through the problem in order to get to the teaching. So here's what happened with Alex and Alice in Wonderland.

Living in Wonderland

Times were great; actually, they always seemed to start great. At this point, there was no better feeling than to be in the place where we were and with the people we loved and respected the most. It was purely an absolute wonder worshipping with our new church family.

I simply could not imagine life getting any better than what my family and I were experiencing. I felt free. Finally we had found a place to grow and learn Scripture in a deeper, more meaningful way. The pastor possessed an incredible amount of wisdom—far beyond my ability to comprehend most times, but somehow it all made perfect sense.

My wife felt safe and secure; our business was thriving; we were able to contribute to the ministry monetarily; and as a result, we could see a bright future ahead. All was good in a place where our gifts could make room for us—a sort of minister/musicians paradise for me, and stability for my wife. Yes, we had truly arrived in "Wonderland."

The first year was awesome as we participated in the growth and the development of the ministry. My wife and family had been well-received; and as I have already mentioned, I had become so close to the pastor, he invited me to speak on his daily radio show. He saw something in me (he was on assignment from God), and I was kind of his pupil being tutored for greater service in the kingdom of God. I must make mention that I was not his only student; he had quite a few who desired to learn the wisdom that came from this man. Though many ears heard the spoken colossal nuggets of truth that came from his lips; at the time, I simply felt like his favorite target because so much emphasis and attention was placed on me for my continual growth and development. As a result, problems with jealousy quickly began heating up.

Nevertheless, I was happy; even though I was aware that jealousy was brewing. I was at the point on picking and choosing my battles for the sake of myself and my family. I mean, we had already endured so much, and I was determined to be happy for as long as I could possibly be. So when I say that the problems could not be helped, I want you to know that I really tried to stay happy. I tried to remember that this Pastor said that God had sent me there for him and for the church family. He said he did not know to what extent, but that God had sent me there… and all of us were about to find out exactly what that meant—in the worst way.

The Wonder in "Wonderland"

"Miracle," "phenomenon," "marvel," "sensation" and "curiosity" are excellent synonyms to describe the word wonder. Three additional terms not mentioned in this list that I believe not only define the word wonder but also embody the totality of that word opposite of its gratifying feeling. Of these three words: "surprise," "astonishment," and "spectacle," in my mind, "spectacle" reigns supreme.

A Ministering Moment

In I Corinthians 4, the Apostle Paul penned under the inspiration of the Holy Spirit, "Let a man so account of us, as of the ministers of Christ, and stewards of the mysteries of God. 2Moreover it is required in stewards, that a man be found faithful" (vv. 1, 2).

In this same chapter, Paul describes to the church at

Chapter 6: God's Boot Camp

Corinth that it was a small thing to him that he should be judged by the very people to whom he had ministered. He mentioned:

> "That knowing nothing by himself; qualified him as just" and to "judge nothing before the time until the Lord come."

Paul was dealing with gifted people who were obviously puffed up in pride because of that to which they were privy. They were speaking in tongues and prophesying and became unmanageable, and Paul had to remind them in verses 7 and 8:

> "…who maketh thee to differ from another? and what hast thou that thou didst not receive? now if thou didst receive it, why dost thou glory, as if thou hast not received it? 8Now ye are full, now ye are rich, ye have reigned as kings without us: and I would to God ye did reign, that we also might reign with you" (KJV).

In verses 9 and 10 the apostle Paul adds,

> "For I think that God hath set forth us the apostles last, as it were appointed to death: for we are made a spectacle unto the world, and to angels, and to men. 10We are fools for Christ's sake, but ye are wise in Christ; we are weak, but ye are strong; ye are honorable, but we are despised" (KJV).

In these verses, Paul is subscribing that he and the rest of the apostles are nothing more than exhibits or spectacles for Christ's sake—even though he had instructed them in the things of God.

Notice the underlined emphasis on humility required to exist in this place of elevation. In other words, Paul could now chasten those who were proud because he himself had to be humbled:

> "Being defamed, we entreat: we are made as the filth of the world, and are the offscouring of all things unto this day" (1 Corinthians 4:13; KJV).

Paul was trying to warn the people of the inevitable shame that was about to come upon his return (v. 14); however, verse 15 lets us know that an instructor was needed for this daunting job of humbling the saints at Corinth in truth. God had given Paul this responsibility to be carried out with love and humility.

As I recall our days at this ministry, I can recall this pastor conveying the following words to me: "Being humble does not necessarily equate to being mute." I did not know it at the time and neither did he, but God was about to see if I could be found loving, humble, and faithful as a steward by making me a spectacle—while breaking down the pride that existed in this church like Paul did in Corinth. My friends, this task did not come easy.

Merry-go-round and Around

Much time had passed since the first day we had arrived in "Wonderland." We were having so much spiritual fulfillment, we felt like we were riding a perpetual carousel of joy going around and round. We were going from Sunday service, to Bible study and other mid-week events, to Saturday rehearsals, to Sunday services, and then starting all over again. We simply could not get enough.

The question was: when will "Wonderland" stop? In truth, I could not tell at the time. We certainly didn't have any quandaries with it; but God knew. And indeed, the merry-go-round did eventually stop. Thankfully, it didn't stop suddenly; nonetheless, the carousel of joy eventually came to a full stop.

The process started inconspicuously through natural se-

Chapter 6: God's Boot Camp

cession, until one morning in Sunday school, our happiness was threatened. My wife noticed it right away, but I wasn't having it. I was trying to savor every moment I could; but I was no fool, it was happening.

My pastor taught a highly concentrated class that was a very important intricate part of the ministry. He was well-known for his brilliant mind and his wisdom in theology as well as apologetics. Attending this class was like sitting in an Ivy League school on Sunday mornings. My pastor was the professor, and not many comments were made because he was quite intimidating. By becoming one of his star pupils, I was expected to answer difficult questions whenever he posed them.

My pastor really thought the world of me. He would often call my home and ask, "Where did you learn this anointed truth in the Word without having attended seminary?" Of course I would always, without fail, give that glory to God and never take any credit for myself. Somehow, that answer never was enough for him. Let me further explain. I would be the only one who would tell him in love where he was wrong in his supposed truth; which, in time, became what is known as dogmatism. He somehow felt as though I was being disrespectful to him after he would ask questions, and I would answer with a truth he did not like. Sadly, our relationship became like a "David and Saul" relationship.

We would go up and down, round and round, back and forth, while agreeing or disagreeing. However, I genuinely loved and respected him like a father in the ministry. I guess that is why things became "out of joint;" he saw me as a son.

While I was shaking in my boots, hoping that he would stop calling my name to answer questions, he would humor everyone else with pastor jargon, employing a tactic of belittling me in the process as he did to so many good men in that church. He would make comments like:

- "I know he knows the answer!"
- "He thinks he's smarter than me!"
- "I don't know who he thinks he is!"
- "You ain't nothing!" (Excuse my Ebonics)

The truth is, I did not know a lot of those answers. Sometimes I didn't even know what he was talking about! This disparagement went on for quite some time and was becoming more cumbersome every Sunday. Ultimately, his tactics led to more serious complications within the ministry.

While he was getting settled in downgrading me before the people, those who were secretly jealous of our now "Paul and Timothy" relationship were surreptitiously cheering him on. Members would witness the things he said to me through teaching, and sometimes he would even burst out at me while preaching, citing that God told him to do it because of the level of my anointing. Sure I believed that excuse, but the church members did not understand what was going on. Subsequently, they too began making statements to me, like, "Look at him. Why does he have to dress so nice all the time? Why is his hair always cut so nice and neat? Is he gay? They would even question my wife, who would frequently sit a few rows from the front, as to why I had to sit up front and not her!

What the people did not know about how I dressed was that I only had two suits and a blazer, but I had learned how to make it work. What they additionally did not know was that the reason why my hair was always neatly trimmed and cut was because I was my own barber, saving money I didn't have. Last, but not least, I guess they could not see that I had a beautiful wife whom I dearly loved, so obviously I wasn't gay; she was sitting on the third row. This kind of activity progressively began spiraling out of control. Week after week people were coming out against me seemingly everywhere the more we went to worship.

Jealousy and pride smothered so many people, and the

Chapter 6: God's Boot Camp

pastor's family was no exception. His wife and daughter spoke to my detriment, convincing him of his lingering suspicion that I was prideful by escalating his arrogance. They managed to twist my stance on truth's foundation sociologically through deception and manipulation by way of the pastor. The pastor began to accuse me of insubordination and abruptly became irate with my supposed pride.

This entire episode was based on a prophecy given by God through my pastor to me, and the Word of the Lord said to me, "Kevin, humble yourself, but humility doesn't mean you're to be mute!" What I found fascinating was a mere suggestion that God was giving me the fortitude to act within His authority, while demanding and requiring me to remain humble was overwhelming. I had become the spectacle (promotion, hallelujah!).

The more God would humble me before the people, the more intense they became with their hatred toward me. They obviously thought they understood the prophecy, but they didn't. God was saying to me, "Don't be mute; rather, tell them the truth in love." At that time, I was becoming what God had been trying to show me all along. The reason I had experienced so many heartaches and pains was because:
"it was required in stewardship, that a man be found faithful… but as for me personally, it matters little that I should be put on trial by you; that I should be investigated and questioned…" (1 Corinthians 4:3; AMP).

They thought I was proud, and with that understanding, they thought they were doing God a favor by humbling me. In all actuality, they were really assisting God in my promotion. (People, stay humble and consistent when men revile you.)

Some people began calling me names; and when they thought my wife should sit up front, they would make comments to her like: "You're the anointed one, not him." "You deserve to sit up front, not him."

The pastor was no stranger to these attacks because his

wife and daughter had already persuaded him that I was the enemy. His daughter seemed enraged with jealousy as she felt threatened by my gift of singing. She was the praise and worship leader, and a few times I sang in her place so my musical ability became a serious issue. Many were for me, and many were against me. The ones who were for me never said anything to me—unless it was behind closed doors.

People were frightened, but they would somehow always tell me I was right by standing for truth. The more I humbled myself, the hotter things became. When I walked into church in full confidence in God, they didn't like it. They were unsettled by my confidence, which they habitually mistook for pride. I was on an out-of-control merry-go-round, and I couldn't get off.

I Had to Be the One

I had to be the one cynical, factual or even rhetorical
I am the one from birth, the day I entered the earth.

I am the one, this I had to be, that's the reason why I'm me.
I'm the one, can't I see, God cleared the road paved for me.

    Faith is my vehicle—sweet ride I see
    But sometimes I go astray and pay the penalty.

    The one I am, not damned—but blessed;
    God has me where He wants; I'm under arrest.

    Around and around and away I go—
    Where will it end? Only He really knows.

So faith is the key and sometimes hard to see,
    But that how it's different just being me.

The Ending of a Matter

Weeks passed, and things were getting hotter and hotter. Unfortunately "my church" had begun boiling over, going completely out of control.

I was sure God would vindicate me, but as to how He would achieve this milestone, I was not certain. I was badly beaten, and in need of daily encouragement. My wife was the forerunner in this area, even while having her own massive degree of difficulty, coping with these strange happenings. All of the denigration was beginning to get to her, but somehow she managed to tough it out with me.

Every now and then, those who spoke to me in secret because they didn't want the heat on them, did their part as well. There were, after all, some beautiful individuals at the church, and we loved them dearly. Even until this day, two of them, Tim and Angel Rollins, have become our most coveted friends. But even they could not stop what would end horrifically, but unanimously for my good.

The Ending

I was always being misquoted or misunderstood. Everything I said or did was frowned upon. If I ministered to someone privately, the story changed by the time it was repeated to the pastor. Through all of this gossiping and backbiting, I remained faithful to God and my church. However, my faithfulness did not matter for the pastor's wife had seen enough. She and her daughters were constantly talking in the pastor's ear, and tension mounted between them.

One sunny Sunday, I was sitting in the front with the rest of the ministers where I had been told to sit since the day I arrived. The church was packed that day, and all seemed well for the moment. The time had come for the pastor to start his message, and he suddenly got up and went in on me. His tirade was a repeat in the worst way of what he would do to me in the

Chapter 6: God's Boot Camp

Sunday school class; only this time, it was in front of the entire congregation. He began rebuking me, as he called it, making comments like:

- "Who do you think you are?"
- "Why are you sitting there like you know it all?"
- "Answer me!"

    I had no clue my pastor was talking to me because the sun was shining so bright in his face, I couldn't see his eyes. I honestly was not sure he was spewing out at me, until he said, "I'm talking to you, Kevin!"
    "You think you're smarter than me? I was smarter than you when I was eighteen than you are now."
    "You're nothing to me. You're stupid. Your momma stupid."
    His rant continued on and on. I can't make this stuff up! Meanwhile, one of his daughters who was sitting up front near me chanted, "Get him pastor; get him." What she started, the church members continued. So I did what any normal person would do under those circumstances. I got up, went to go get my wife, but I left alone without her. The whole scenario had finally gotten to her; she was confused and frozen in time... To her, there was no reasonable explanation.

> "O the depth of the riches both of the wisdom and knowledge of God! How unsearchable are his judgments, and his ways past finding out! For who hath known the mind of the Lord? Or who hath been his counselor?" (Romans 11:33, 34; KJV).

    A singer songwriter, VaShawn Mitchell wrote: "I will seek You until I find You, for the rest of my life I'll keep running after You!"

Even though I was desperately hurting inwardly, I knew I had come too far with God. If it took the rest of my life, I wasn't giving up. This time was not like the others. I had grown with God; and I had battle scars to prove it. I was closer to Him than I had ever been before, and I was here to stay. Although I didn't know the mind of Christ, I was persuaded to follow Him where He led me.

The End of Days

Several days had passed after my exodus relieving myself of the menacing chants of flesh eaters. I dare to think what might have happened had I stayed any longer than I did; nevertheless, after a brief period of recuperation, I returned with my entire family on a Wednesday night. As it has been for quite some time, the church was thriving. The pastor was increasing in popularity, and his radio show was peaking. His pride was off the charts because of his success. When my wife and I came in, we had to find a seat wherever we could; the sanctuary was jam-packed on a Wednesday night.

Needless to say, all eyes were on me even though we were sitting in the back of the church. I had hoped to talk with the pastor to see if we could iron out this difficulty, but I wasn't prepared for what happened when his wife was asked to speak. Upon taking the microphone, she began speaking to the congregants. She made eye contact with me while praising her husband for the man of God he was. Back and forth she went, saying how deserving he was of praise.

As I listened to her talk about praising him, in my mind I was thinking, What? Where is all this going? She suddenly began to make a case that anyone who was disrespecting her pastor-husband by walking out on him when he was rebuking him would meet serious consequences. They would have to deal with her!

I have no doubt that everybody knew she was talking to

Chapter 6: God's Boot Camp

me. She became so irritated, enraged, and beside herself that she challenged me to an open fight right then and there. When she issued that public challenge, I was through—DONE!

I looked at my wife and motioned for us to leave. While I was saying this to my wife, the pastor's wife was chanting, "Come on, come on! I'll fight you now! I'm like Peter; I will cut your ear off!"

I was thinking, Are you serious? Is this even real? Does anyone see this happening?

What was even more incredible was the fact that the people were cheering her on.

As I looked at my wife, she said, "Baby, why don't you go up there and talk to the pastor?"

"Um…honey, don't you see what's going on in here?"

"Yes, Kevin, but…"

"But what?"

"I think you should go up there and try to talk with him."

So against my own will and at the request of my wife, we started making our way toward the front of the church. There I told his wife that I had no interest in fighting her, but the deacons had already surrounded me like they were going to jump me. I then looked at the pastor. He was sitting and never stood for one moment. "Pastor," I said, "I need to speak with you."

Yes, all of this was happening while the church service was supposedly going on.

As he was sitting there taking the stance of a king on this throne, he said, "We have nothing to talk about. All you need to do is kneel down and apologize to me for walking out on me."

I could not believe the blatant pride this man was displaying. The look on my wife's face suggested that she now clearly saw what these people in leadership were about. She burst into tears, and then I became angry. I grabbed my wife's hand to leave. While the pastor was telling me to beg forgiveness for his embarrassing me, the pastor's wife was whispering in my wife's ear, "Leave him…" But Stephanie did not listen, and we could not get out of there fast enough. As we were leaving via the middle aisle, people were excoriating us and chanting, "You demons!" "Devils!"

A Ministry Moment: The Power of Humility

Humility in the Greek is the feminine noun an-ä-vä. When applied to God, humility describes the side of Him that is gentle. However, God is also masculine as in eks-ü-sē-ä (meaning "powerful") and yet gentle as in lowliness within the person of Christ. This denotes Christ's willfully submitting under God, as He was God in the flesh.

The Bible describes humility as "meekness, lowliness and absence of self." The Greek word translated humility in Colossians 3:12 and elsewhere literally means "lowliness of mind," so we see that humility is a heart attitude—not merely an outward demeanor.

The meaning of power: masculine, having authority and yet the word can be in the feminine when applied to submitting under authority. Also archē denotes the authority granting the power.

The meaning of humility: "feminine, meekness or lowliness"

When considering being successful in the kingdom of God, one has to possess humility that must be governed by power. After all, power alone produces pride. While some may exude an outward show of humility, they still can possess a heart full of pride and arrogance; these are they who will never operate in nor inherit the kingdom of God.

Jesus said that those who are "poor in spirit" would have the kingdom of heaven; being poor in spirit (which is another word for humility) means that "only those who admit to an absolute bankruptcy of spiritual worth will inherit eternal life."

Chapter 6: God's Boot Camp

Therefore, humility is a prerequisite to power for the Christian in three areas:

- It gives us access to God. "Therefore, being justified by faith, we have peace with God through our Lord Jesus Christ: By whom also we have access by faith into this grace wherein we stand" (Romans 5:1, 2 KJV).
- It gives us grace ("unmerited favor") with God; through the progression of time explaining humility's full potential, thereby escaping God's resistance and positioning us for elevation.
- It gives us the promise of possessing the kingdom of God; "Blessed are the poor in spirit: for theirs is the kingdom of heaven." (Matt. 5:3 KJV)

In other words, like Christ retained authority through lowliness and gentleness and having all authority (power),

"He still made himself of no reputation. He took upon himself the form of a servant, and was made in the likeness of men; and being found in fashion as a man, he humbled himself, and became obedient unto death, even the death of the cross." (Phil. 2:7 KJV)

"Wherefore God also hath highly exalted him, and given him a name which is above every name." He promised us the same in Matthew 5:3 through "the power of humility." In other words, God is saying that through the power of humility, happy are those who are lowly and depleted of power because through their humility, they will have the God-given right, power, and authority to rule over a kingdom.

I wanted to remain humble in this situation, but I simply did not know how. I wanted to be successful in the kingdom of God; I wanted to be meek and lowly and absent of myself. I had no desire to exude pride and arrogance; I wanted grace and favor.

WAITING ON GOD

I felt powerless, lowliness of heart, and bankrupt. Nevertheless, in this moment of moments that was qualifying us to give us the right, the power, and the authority to rule over a kingdom, God showed up for Stephanie and me in the most unlikely manner. You see, God did not want me to run as I had done before.

To ensure that I would not run, as we were exiting the building to go to our car, I did not notice that our car was the only one blocked in the entire parking lot. We had cars blocking us from front to back, and side to side. We had to go back in and face the music!

So we gathered ourselves and walked back into the building. This time we re-entered the church through the side entrance leading to the front of the sanctuary. As we were walking in, we could hear the pastor's son addressing his mother, his father, and the church, and this is what he said:
Church, WE ARE WRONG! This is not Christ-like; we are wrong! This man has done nothing to us nor has he done anything wrong!

Through the pastor's son, God validated me before the pastor, his wife, his daughters, and the entire church. The pastor sensed that he too should concede, so he took full advantage of the situation by asking me to kneel while he laid hands on me, in an effort to save face and "sort of" restore me. He then told the church that the issue was concluded, and that they should leave me alone. For all of this showing from him, God had already worked His work through the pastor's own son.

After that, my wife and I found it utterly embarrassing and humanly difficult to remain at the ministry, but we stayed as we did at the former ministry. Our obedience to God had cost us a great deal, but the spiritual elevation and illumination made the problems all worth it! Christ had now become the single-most, important focal point of our lives; we would now have to take His yoke upon us and learn more of Him.

Although life was now good and the warfare seemingly

Chapter 6: God's Boot Camp

over, one day while sitting in service, my wife and I simultaneously heard the voice of God instructing us to move on. We turned to each other, and with a humble sigh of relief, we exited the building. My wife and I moved from the place of "Wonderland" to finding rest on our way to the wilderness. With no one left but us and our four walls…it would be a year before we heard from God again!

These Four Walls

These four walls that contain our being,
They try to entrap our mind.
Am yet we are present before these walls,
We fail to be in the midst.
What about these four walls that claim to be as the white snow?
But only to reveal the stain of blood. Oh, these walls!
Yes! Four they are; we understand this is true,
But our mind, our mind, and oh, these walls.
Each night we stare at these four walls,
Forced to question our being;
And we travel to our depth only to search
Ourselves through and through…for what?
I don't know, and yet we search to find.
What about these four walls?
They connect at four corners, joined together
Forming a never-ending story,
But there is a door within these walls…
Maybe we should go out the way we came in.

Chapter 7: We Found Rest

Contained within the book of Hebrews is the summation of resting in Christ. The purpose of the epistle was to reassure Jewish believers that their faith in Christ Jesus as the Messiah was secure and legitimate. Also, the book was intended to prepare the Hebrews for the impending disaster of the Roman destruction of Jerusalem. The temple, with its system of animal sacrifices and the office of priest, would soon be done away with, as Jesus had foretold.

Hebrews 4:9 says, "There remaineth therefore a rest to the people of God" (KJV).

Our faith in Christ Jesus was now secure, and nothing or no one could ever change that fact. Like in biblical times, God challenged what man perceived of Him in many awe-striking, jaw-dropping ways. Now, we too had seen God move in our lives on a level that many biblical patriarchs themselves had witnessed.

Stephanie and I were now in need of that rest spoken of in Hebrews 4:9. Though a full year was approaching without hearing from above, God allowed us to heal and bond together as a family. He had even prospered us; yet, not hearing from Him at all on our way to the next ministry seemed somewhat strange after experiencing God on an elevated level and now in a place of rest.

Hebrews 4:10 says, "For he that is entered into his rest, he also hath ceased from his own works, as God did from his" (KJV).

The work was done. For the moment, God had apparently paused His training with us. His silence was an indicator of His rest from the previous work, and that we should rest and prepare for the impending work that would surely come again. You see, God rested, I rested, and Stephanie rested. We both knew that soon it would be time to go back to work, but now it was time for sanctuary.

Have you ever been in a situation where everything was going fairly good, and you really didn't feel the pressures of life that existed around you? It's almost like you're in a cocoon, and as long as you're in there, you remain protected, nourished, and you can grow.

The beginning of our year of rest was exactly that. God had provided us with a covering that had safeguarded us from potential harm, while we healed from the above-mentioned events at the previous ministry. He had even begun dealing with us prophetically frequently in dreams/visions and interpretations of such, which would prove to be very important for where we would end up.

I must say again that life was really good. Certainly not hearing from God on a consistent basis was obviously difficult, but we found joy, peace and solitude in each other, our children, and the business. Our profession led to many new endeavors unimagined. We began developing new business ideas; we renovated our salon with new flooring, styling stations, paint and décor; we initiated new policies and became more efficient in running the business; we even implemented new marketing strategies and started doing more photo shoots.

Stephanie's work soon graced magazines including Upscale, Passion, Hype Hair and Sophisticate's Black Hair Magazine—to name a few. I became the quintessential business pro-

Chapter 7: We Found Rest

fessional, and together we were unstoppable. Yes, we were blessed with no signs of any kind of unwanted activity from the spirit world that could amass against me and my family. At that time, we had the perfect situation with each other, with family, very few friends, and our business.

Our landlord was equally blessed, and he passed it on to us. We were located on a busy stretch of highway that demanded that we pay more for the location we occupied; but God gave my wife favor with the owner of the property. He gave us a price for which others in that area paid double and sometimes triple!

God Speaks Again

> When life hurts you, your brand of truth becomes your philosophy! Your vision is then compromised, thereby dictating your now reality. We must at all cost allow Christ in through the Word of God to renew our minds.—Kevin L. Lipsey, Sr.

This profound statement came within a revelatory moment—even when things were going so great. The implication is that though things were great, Stephanie's mind as well as my mind had to be rehabilitated. It was imperative at some point for us to re-enter the ministry source which God had chosen for our continual development.

As it turns out, God had apparently selected our next destination, and one day while working at the salon, I met the liaison while buying lunch for my wife. I was at Wendy's when suddenly a middle-aged woman began complimenting me on my hair and how good I looked.

I was thinking, "Is this woman trying to hit on me?" Wow, that's strange.

So she says to me, "Who does your hair?"

I replied, "Me."

She once again compliments me and says, "Wow, it looks really great."

At this point, I was thinking (right or wrong) I needed to stop this cougar-like advance by somehow acknowledging the fact I had a wife. So when she asked me the next question, which was, "What do you do?" I replied, "My wife and I own the hair salon across the street."

Men, you can learn from my experience. Stop potential matters before they happen; however, this meeting quickly turned to what God purposed it to be when I asked her to stop by the salon if she would like to get her hair done.

She then asked, "Are you a Christian?" When I replied that I was, she asked, "Where do you worship?"

When I answered "Nowhere," (Don't forget that Stephanie and I were at rest, meaning we were temporarily out of church) she followed me to the salon where she met my wife, inquired about getting her hair done, and left us with an open invitation to come to her church.

When I asked her what kind of church it was, she replied in an interesting manner. "Non-denominational, but different! Just come, and you'll see for yourself. I think it would be good for you and your wife."

How could I know that God was re-entering us into ministry, and He worked His will through an unknown woman and a purposeful encounter that day at a Wendy's. Maybe Stephanie and I needed a change of scenery, and certainly it was good to see and hear that God was back speaking to us again. I wondered what more He would have to say…

The Prophetic Season

The prophetic occurrences continued, and though meeting this woman was somewhat of a happening, nothing could prepare us for what we would witness when visiting this nameless woman's church. Some time had passed since we had met the woman at

Chapter 7: We Found Rest

Wendy's, and one morning my wife had a dream that we visited the church. While we were there, the pastor called us up to the front and prophesied to us. He said that I was one of God's generals. Once again, God spoke the same words! Then she awakened and told me the dream, adamant that we should get dressed and go to the church.

Upon our arrival, we noticed right away the difference "tag" she had expressed, and "different" really gave no justice to what we would experience. In fact, the word "odd" was more or less the proper term to use when describing this church. Nothing about it was quite like anything I had ever seen. But true to my wife's dream, the ministry was prophetic, and the pastor was a prophet/seer.

The music was not as appealing to me as a musician and a singer/songwriter. I was floored that they had very few singers and little to no musicianship. They sang songs that nobody knew, and oftentimes they did not seem to know them either. They called it singing "prophetically"—not to mention they sang for hours, appearing to have no concept of order and time. The pastor was nowhere to be found, and we discovered he would get to church extremely late because he apparently came from one of their other strange churches out of town. He followed this schedule every Sunday!

His late arrival indeed explained why they sang and carried on for so long. For the record, I'm not saying "strange" because of the prophetic ministry; rather in how they conducted the service. I have shared my first impression of this ministry, and I was thinking in my mind, *Oh, I know precisely what God is going to have me do here. Yes, I can see it clearly.* However, little did I know that this so-called strange activity was exactly what my wife and I needed.

You see, we had reflected while at rest, that in one church, it was about the man (pastor); his family; occasionally no order and trying to achieve it, all the while hurting others who were in the ministry. Hurt people hurt other people. The second church was about order and excellence that took center stage and the man and the people serving the man—the pastor. He was so paranoid because he did not know if I was a renegade, threatening to go against his brand of order.

The third ministry was power-hungry through knowledge. "The more knowledge you have, the more power you have." The pastor used this knowledge in a lethal way through what is called "social psychological manipulation," which is essentially getting what he wanted through a deceptive influence over the church. The focus was also the pursuit of fame and becoming so world renowned that pride ensued; too much focus was on the man (pastor) as the alpha male of knowledge and also on his family's swaying him to supply their needs through the people.

At this new ministry, it was the opposite. They had no concern for the man (pastor) or his family, no striving for order and excellence, no pride that I could detect, and no trying to be world renowned. Their only thing was "the prophetic," and lots of it.

Naturally Stephanie and I were on the pastor's radar from the moment he spotted us; and the prophetic words soon followed after he would preach the message. I had heard people prophesy before, but when I tell you that this man was on a different level, he was. Two of his first prophetic utterances spoken to us were the catalyst that spawned several prophetic occurrences. Our lives would drastically change, and a new course would be charted.

This is important in that Pastor Hall sadly departed to be with the Lord, but before He did, God used him powerfully to point us in the right direction prophetically. I will only share the prophetic words pertinent to this story's unfolding.

Recounting this story brings back so many memories gone by, and yet the joy of knowing Pastor Hall and how truly awesome God is was now about to manifest in our lives. That is

Chapter 7: We Found Rest

what makes what I'm going to share with you is so special. Here are two excerpts from Stephanie's journal of spoken prophetic words:

Prophetic Word #1: Pastor called on us again. First he called me [Stephanie] and then told me to bring Kevin. He spoke that God showed him that everything I was trying to do would fail, and nothing I touched would prosper. I was good at what I do (hair); however, we couldn't get anything through our hands. The reason was because people were praying against the business and me, and they were jealous of me because of Kevin.

The Enemy wasn't after me; he was after Kevin. He wanted to attack me to keep Kevin off-track, but God wanted the pastor to anoint me [Stephanie]. He told Kevin that he saw land, trees, and that property was in his heart. He saw him trying to produce something; his career was okay and the Lord said that this day Kevin is approved.

Prophetic Word #2: Pastor Hall called Kevin up today. He said that God showed him Kevin praying, asking the Lord for direction because Kevin wanted to make sure he was in God's will. The Lord showed the pastor a document that had already passed through Kevin's hand with his personal information on it. The document stated that Kevin had been declined, but the Lord was approving him at a bank; it was already at someone's desk.

We were so happy, joyful, dumbfounded and confused all rolled-up in one. Don't get me wrong, those things had not yet occurred, but what was that all about? I didn't know! Now the house situation was already in progress. The pastor had just confirmed God's take on the matter, and we were happy about that confirmation. However, the other part left us unsure about everything around us; still, we moved forward anyway.

Going to the Promise

Up until that point, we had been living in a two-bedroom apartment and occasionally, we would have all the kids over, totaling six people. Even though it was good, you can imagine how crowded the living conditions were with all of the children there.

However, what's interesting is how we got there. It all happened one Sunday evening after church when the six of us had finished dinner and had begun relaxing around the house. Suddenly, I heard a bang at the door, and a person began yelling, "Fire! Fire!" Within seconds, everything was total pandemonium! I am talking about fire trucks and paramedics arriving within minutes. I barely had time to react in safely getting my family out of the apartment. We narrowly escaped with our lives, and while in a moment of silent gratitude, we watched in disbelief as flames devoured our little abode.

In total shock in the freezing cold, we retreated to a nearby hotel where we lodged for three days. With God's help, we found a rental home where we stayed for a year, and we then moved to an apartment community closer to the business. This displacement all happened right before we left the previous ministry.

We began inquiring about our credit, and with the word from " the Lord," Stephanie and I quickly stepped out on faith, not renewing our lease, and moved into an extended stay where we could sojourn until further notice from God. Living at the extended stay was a test of our faith. We were surrounded by people who played loud music, cursed, and used foul language. They were outright heathens, which made it difficult to maintain our faith and a family structure in a one-room, two bed habitation, but we are the "Lipseys"—no matter where we dwell. Oh, the room number was "111," and in our minds, it represented the Father, the Son, and the Holy Ghost—a constant reminder

Chapter 7: We Found Rest

that through the trials of life, God was with us.

One day when visiting friends, God gave me an open vision of a subdivision while leaving their home. I asked Stephanie to drive because I wanted to be clear about the location where God was leading me. While she was driving in the general area, I noticed the subdivision God had displayed to me in the vision. I said to Stephanie, "Turn here; this is it."

Once we entered the neighborhood, immediately I saw a great number of trees, and Stephanie commented: "These are some large homes…baby, they're way out of our price range."

"Baby, just drive…" I answered, "God can do anything! I want to see something."

I saw that the houses were spaced out and each property had land—exactly like Pastor Hall had said. As we were looking at the houses, we noticed signs on the front lawn of some selected homes that read "$10,000 Bonus!" We inwardly pondered about the signs, which caused us to further investigate.

The next day, we returned to the subdivision to inquire about the homes. We met with the agent on the property who asked if we had our own agent. Of course, we responded, "No!" In the back of my mind I was thinking that my credit and my church was still yet determined—not to mention I had no money. Then the property agent recommended someone and instructed us to come back at six o'clock that evening to meet the agent.

When we met her, something peculiar happened. She brought along her husband, who happened to be a pastor! We know immediately that God was doing something, but what?! We introduced ourselves and proceeded to view two homes with the $10,000-bonus sign on the lawn. As Stephanie and the agent looked at the houses, her husband and I began sharing the "good news" about the Lord.

The first house was okay, but Stephanie wanted to view the next house. While walking up the driveway of that house, God spoke to me in a clear voice and said, "Tell Stephanie to choose one of these houses." So I told Stephanie exactly as I had been instructed. She looked at me, smiled, and then asked, "God told you to tell me that?

"Yes."

"Okay," said Stephanie.

Certainly, all that was happening seemed strange to me; nevertheless, I obeyed the voice of the Lord anyway.

Once inside, my wife and the agent were going on and on about the features of the house. Unbeknown to me, Stephanie had a secret list before the Lord, listing specific features she wanted in a house, and this property had them all! The house was complete with hardwood floors, ceramic tile, stainless steel appliances, his and her walk-in closets, and much more. Apparently, my wife's desires were no secret to God. I believe this was the reason why He had Stephanie choose.

Meanwhile, the pastor and I were so engulfed in the things of God that I did not notice my wife had agreed to put a contract on the house with "no money, undetermined credit, and with only a word from the Lord!" I never made it past the foyer. The next thing I knew, we were in the front office, signing papers, while I continued to exchange stories about my experiences with God.

As it turned out, the money from those $10,000-bonus signs could be used as closing costs and/or upgrades to the home. We were ecstatic—although we didn't have a dime to our name. As we were finishing up the paperwork, and as I was coming out of my glorious conversation with the pastor, the agent explained to us that we only needed a check for the earnest deposit of $1,000. We didn't know how we would get it, but we told her confidently and in faith that we would have it the next day.

While riding back to the hotel, Stephanie and I sat in complete silence; we were in total awe of what God was preparing for us. Was this a dream? Was it real? That prophecy was really manifesting. Was I really approved by God? The very idea

Chapter 7: We Found Rest

that something of that magnitude could be done was such a far-fetched notion to me—well, a little. I knew our credit at that time was not in our favor, and we were living in an extended stay.

By now, the bad and the ugly were long gone, but I assure you never forgotten. The next step was to secure a mortgage loan or at least inquire about one, but before we did that, we shared the news of what God was doing with a few friends and some family members. This divulging turned out to be a bad idea—but one that couldn't be helped. We had called one family member whom I will refer to as, "Mr. Stacks."

"Why?" Well, Mr. Stacks had a great deal of stacks (money). We had no preconceived predatory ideas in reaching out to him, but certainly letting Mr. Stacks know what you've accomplished with God at the helm couldn't hurt! "Could it?!!"

After talking with Mr. Stacks, surprisingly he was quite happy for us and quickly suggested that we use his people. You know the drill: "Have your people call my people." He ended up giving us the earnest money we needed for the house. Our faith and trust in God was strengthening as we witnessed His opening doors before our eyes.

A day later Mr. Stacks' loan officer checked my credit score because Stephanie's was somewhat challenged. I discovered that my credit wasn't bad; I simply didn't have any. On that basis, I was rejected, and we couldn't get a house. They explained to me my score wasn't bad at all, that I needed some negatives to fall off, and I needed to open another line of credit—all while God somehow miraculously gave me over one hundred points, and then we could see about getting a house. "Seems like a lot, huh?" And all this needed to happen, as Mr. Stacks' people conveyed to me, in 30 days by the time they pulled my credit again.

My dear wife said (in Ebonics), "Baby, ain't no way, A hundred points?!!"

I responded, "Baby, God can do anything. God said I was approved."

"Okay," Stephanie replied with a saying that she had: "That's on you and God."

Instead of responding, I answered inwardly. Lord, I know You're going to do this for me and my family. You told me I was approved. Finally allow something worthy to happen for me, so I can do something noble for my family—rather than taking them on a ride-along through my unpredictable and complex life.

Well, in about twenty days after praying and working our due diligence (being responsible and paying things that we owed within reach), God caused amazing things to happen. What I needed to fall off, well, they fell off. One company called me and said they were taking themselves off of my credit report. Yes, this company simply called out of nowhere. The bank I went through to finance my car and was delinquent in paying several times fell off too. I had called a man whom I had befriended at the bank and told him what I was trying to do. That good man took everything reporting as a late payment off of my credit and replaced it with paid as agreed. Please don't tell me God can't do a thing!

Stephanie and I were literally in awe of what our God was doing, but it didn't stop there. Those hundred points I needed came out to be about one hundred twenty points, which propelled my score well beyond what we could have ever imagined in only twenty days! My credit was now "A-1!"

Consequently, after talking with Mr. Stack's people again, I found that I had been approved by the bank and that I was qualified to get a house for more than $269,000. The house that my wife had chosen was only $215,900 with more bells and whistles than most of the homes in that subdivision—but for less. The blessing was just seven minutes away. God approved me exactly as Pastor Hall had prophesied.

Now this account may not seem much to you, but to me, our new house would be the first one I had ever owned. I was so happy that I cried. I began reminiscing about the time when I was a little boy roller skating in the house I had loved as a child.

Chapter 7: We Found Rest

What a momentous occasion—a far cry from the days of hurting from the things I had lost along the way.

A Ministering Moment

> "God can do a thing in our lives without our trying to cause a thing to happen." Kevin L. Lipsey, Sr.

I want to share about the in-depth process of acquiring our home. Oftentimes we hear many testimonies touting our God as the awesome wonder of the universe because something good has taken place in our lives.

I certainly agree that God is awesome; however, I would like to focus on a subject infrequently mentioned—the dishonest things Christians confidently do while attaching God's name to their proposed blessing. The above quotation suggests that unless He desires, God rarely needs our help in doing anything in our lives. Yet most Christians conveniently assist God through dishonesty, while giving Him the credit for a seeming miracle birthed from lies.

> "The truth weakens in a moment of desperation of a thing desired, we simply will not tell the truth!"—Kevin L. Lipsey, Sr.

The most difficult thing for us to come into as humans is the knowledge of truth. We struggle at the least of its rendering, yet if we do not consider performing it, consequently it will indict us. The indictment will bring with it unimaginable charges spiritually, inevitably manifesting fleshly.

At the beginning of this venture, my wife and I demanded truth of ourselves in this home-buying process in order for God to produce the best possible outcome. "His Word!" We gave Him a solid foundation to build upon, which was truth in this matter under consideration—truly, in truth; according to truth of a truth; in reality, in fact, certainly. God didn't need our help, but our part was important to us. We both wanted to be pure and without accusation from our Adversary.

Revelation 12:10 says, "Now is come salvation, and strength, and the kingdom of our God, and the power of his Christ: for the accuser of our brethren is cast down, which accused them before our God day and night" (KJV).

The emphasis here is that our Adversary is not only "… seeking whom he may devour," but he is actively making accusations against us before God daily. Stephanie and I wanted to resist being dishonest and being accused by actively remaining steadfast in our faith that we had so willingly placed in God. Our desire for truth worked big time.

God was maturing us, but we did not know it. Our carnal mind was on the blessing before us; however, considering the many trials we had endured over the years, I got the sense that something was brewing that neither of us could detect nor understand. But for now, we'll enjoy this one.

The Promise (the House)

By now we had begun serious negotiations with the Mortgage Company and bank. We looked forward to closing the deal within a reasonable time frame. God was busy, and we wanted to cash in. Normally these proceeding last about thirty days, but for some unknown reason, though I was approved, this process took two months to close. We had come so far in truth and honesty in this matter, lived in unfavorable conditions, prayed diligently, and the process was held up?! The Devil is a liar! We're going to get this house!

Apparently Mr. Stack's people were stalling to get more money out of the deal; they wanted to go beyond 30 days so they could change their percentage while increasing my rate. God had worked on my credit; it was now A-1, and they wanted to cash

Chapter 7: We Found Rest

in on that fact. One loan officer even called to ask me if I minded if he could "fib" a little to the bank. I replied, "Of course not!" There was no need. He'd even tried to make it seem as though it was going to be difficult to try and get the deal done—all because of money; but the word of the Lord said, "I was approved!" So I instructed him to leave my paperwork as I had given it to him—honest and true. Disclaimer: I must say, I don't think Mr. Stacks had anything to do with his people's business practices.

We went back and forth, up and down, setting up times that we could close the deal. The time was tumultuous with serious warfare implications. Nonetheless, we had to fight to obtain what God had already spoken and confirmed was ours.

Forceful prayers were implemented while supplicating to God to untie the strong hold and remove the stumbling blocks. Tensions were high, we were trying to run a business, we were tired of existing in an extended stay, and everything was beginning to bother us. Nevertheless, we never told the kids what God was doing, but we did take them to see the house several times, encouraging them to dream big and to believe in God. We told family members who had only asked how things were going to see if we would fail. They were jealous along with many so-called friends who were anxious for us to be denied; they didn't want me to have a house that big and nice.

Stemming from the previous ministry when I shared on how people were putting my wife before me, the rumor was that she was buying this house. Supposedly I had somehow manipulated her in a sinister grand scheme to get ahead in life and perhaps now my plot was backfiring on me. I couldn't believe that after things were going so well that God would allow such ominous activity. However, we persevered and believed that "this too would pass;" and that we would prevail. After all of this, more than two months later, I finally got the call that the paperwork was finished.

We went to the closing, and before we could conclude,

the closing attorney came across a discrepancy. Oh, no, what now? He told us his concern for the future of the type of loan we had received. He also mentioned that he didn't understand why, with my credit, I had received the rate that I had gotten.

Of course we were worried, but more importantly, at that time, we were completely worn out. He told us that if we would refinance before a certain period that we would be fine, but we needed to make sure to pay our mortgage on time. I should have suspected something was wrong then, but again we were utterly and completely worn out and ready to move into our new home. After the completion of all paperwork, I was then asked to write a check for the closing cost in the amount of $167, which I was happy to do. Shortly thereafter, we concluded the closing and finally closed on our dream house. Then I received the keys to my very first house ever. We shed tears of joy.

My wife and I literally stormed out of that office so fast, I don't think we even told the attorneys goodbye. We were so overwhelmed with joy that we could hardly wait to finally tell the kids what we had been doing. The way we chose to announce we were moving was quite unique. We took them to the house after we got the keys and told them we were going to see the house one last time. While in the house, they picked out their rooms and were quite happy—not even knowing the outcome and thinking of the possibilities of "what if!" Thinking out loud, we were all decorating the house, picturing what it would be like if we were living there and what we would do. My son even responded, "Man, if only God would give us a house like this!" Of course, we told him that God could do anything, we simply needed to trust and believe in Him.

So after holding the secret for as long as we could, when we were leaving, we told them that we were going to get our belongings.

"What? We can't just put our things in this house!"

Stephanie or I responded, "Yes we can because this is our

Chapter 7: We Found Rest

house!"

"Are you serious?"

"Yes," we said.

Both of our children burst into tears, and ours followed. We wept tears of joy because God had given us a victory!

We moved in right away. We didn't want to spend another painstaking minute, hour, day or night in that extended stay. We gathered what little we had, and that night we slept in our new home. We had no beds, no furniture, and no window treatments, but we didn't care as long as we were together at home.

As you can imagine, everything was beautiful, living in the home God had given to us.

Our children absolutely adored that house and quickly made new friends in the forty-nine-home neighborhood. My wife and I equally, if not more, loved the home and made every attempt to maintain the good times living there would bring—even if only for a few years. That house was like our oasis in the midst of a desert; however, we were not out of the desert, only in an oasis. What happened will be in our next book, but I will leave you with this clue as to what happened: "God told us to leave!"

On a higher note, we were able to contribute in many ways as well as learn a great deal in that prophetic ministry. I would dare say that it was an exchange on our part with the church. For us, it wasn't simply correcting them; it was more about God's removing the final kinks out of us before He would release us in ministry. He would also reveal prophetically through Pastor Hall and others who possessed the gift of prophecy our past experiences, thereby bringing spiritual understanding to what had been mostly our dark days.

As for the church, many of them I did correct, and we grew in bond for many years. The pastor discovered by his own admission that he had some things wrong about God though he possessed a powerful prophetic gift! And so after eight years, we moved on—still continuing our journey in "waiting on God."

Chapter 8:
The Wilderness

In the Word of God, we are told about a story of a people who were once in bondage, then released from that bondage, and then ushered into a wilderness. They proceeded only to complain that the previous bondage didn't seem like repression until they arrived where they were at that moment—in "the wilderness."

Webster's Dictionary describes the word wilderness as "a wild and uncultivated region, as of forest or desert, uninhabited or inhabited only by wild animals." This definition is interesting when compared to the Hebrew rendering of the same word—midvar, which means:

> For forty years God had Israel wander in the "wilderness." Insights into why God had chosen the wilderness for their wanderings can be found in the roots of this word. The root word is davar and is most frequently translated as "a thing or a word." The original picture painted by this word to the Hebrews is the arrangement of things to create order. Speech is an ordered arrangement of words. In the ancient Hebrew mind, words are "things" and are just as "real" as food or other "things." When a word is spoken to another it is "placed in the ears" no different than when

food is given to another it is "placed in the mouth." The Hebrew name Devorah (Deborah) means "bee" and is the feminine form of the word davar. Bees are a community of insects which live in a perfectly ordered arrangement.

The word midvar meaning "wilderness" is actually a place that exists as a perfectly arranged order as its ecosystem is in harmony and balance. By placing Israel in this environment he is teaching them balance, order and harmony.—Jeff A. Benner

This truth in contrast to the more secular view couldn't be clearer when considering what we had been through. 1 Corinthians 2:14, "Now the natural man receives not the things of the Spirit of God: for they are foolishness unto him; and he cannot know them, because they are spiritually judged." The worldly view seems to echo this passage with veracity! Yet because of its truth, our wilderness was quite real. Never could we have known that the wilderness intended would breed such harmony, order and balance; however, in a manner that would cause us to question God in a seemingly chaotic mass. Although we had already experienced massive hardship, this so-called wilderness would indeed be reality for us.

I am reminded of a passage of Scripture which describes God as being pleased to bruise His son. Isaiah 53:10, "Yet it pleased the Lord to bruise him; he hath put him to grief." The word please is the Hebrew word chaphets which means "to delight in, take pleasure in, desire and be pleased with." The word bruise is the word daka; it means "to crush or be crushed, to be contrite or broken."

The previous experiences we encountered over the course of this book to us were likened to dwelling in Egypt; and for Israel, this was bondage! God forewarned them that their disobedience to Him would ultimately cause them to be put into suppression.

Chapter 8: The Wilderness—The Sum Of All Things

It is this suppression that is synonymous in many ways to the Hebrew rendering of bruising, and God the Father was pleased to do so. Oftentimes, God has to implement the suppressions in order to crush our ways, leaving us with the obvious better choice, which is to choose Him. Believe it or not, this is actually LOVE!

The Total Sum of Things: Order, Balance, and Harmony

Though I'm grateful that the previous story turned in our favor due to a prophetic utterance from God through Pastor Hall and that no weapon formed against us was able to prosper, I would be remiss if I did not state that it was far from over. In fact, this story as I have stated, was ultimately about God's maturing us to accomplish His purpose in our life.

This will continue until the day of Jesus Christ according to Philippians 1:6, though we are now in ministry. So if you're looking for some blockbuster ending, then you have failed to capture the true essence of this book.

Let me explain: In the beginning of the book, you were told to "forget what you've been told and of what you think you know" about God. Even knowledge-based theological studies cannot sum Him because what can be known of God can only be given by Him. Since we are subject to His all-knowing wisdom and power, He has to prepare us to either receive or reject Him based on the Fall in the Genesis account.

The Genesis descent of man is often not comprehended by believers worldwide and thus deserves some attention. This is done through trials and lessons that should produce growth and maturity in knowing Him. We are being matured in order that **we may know him**. We cannot know Him from the abyss of ignorance (sin), but we can get to know Him through **relationship, trials, tribulations and time**.

Within these relationship and trials we are subject to

Him, and understanding His ways is not easy because of the gorge stemming from Adam in which we found ourselves. We learn He does things rather different; frankly speaking, it's because He's sovereign! What he wants is to know and commune with us or to have a relationship with us. This appears critical in that an all-knowing God would want to know the thing He created. How can He not know us?

As already stated, this of course, has brought to my understanding the incorrect doctrinal issue facing believers today. Many have caused God's people to err, spawning un-calculative events in the lives of those who are in the pursuit of finding God. What He wants is for us to know that He is love and that He loves us; nevertheless, because of enmity, we were separated and broken apart.

> Enmity is the Greek word echthros; it means "hated, odious, hateful, and hostile or opposing another." It is also used of men as at enmity with God by their sin.

In plain words, our sinful nature caused us to fall so deep while dwelling in this flesh; we were bound to be hostile, opposing, and even hate God! It isn't that He does not know us; rather, He does not understand the hostility or hatred toward Him Who first LOVED us, and He Who is LOVE; therefore, we are apart.

Nonetheless it is because of this love that He is tolerant (full of grace) and did not destroy us, but showed mercy. We are talking about a Holy God, and He had every right! However, His grace and mercy suggested that He would try from a relational perspective to rekindle the lost love caused by enmity. Now I know this might sound irrational, but consider what I shared about my marriage.

One:

Chapter 8: The Wilderness—The Sum Of All Things

I was one with her before time began. I was complete. *Chapter one, page five insert*: I was fully equipped in this meeting, and to me was given everything I needed to endure; again I was whole. Once I reached my earthly starting point, **a part of me would be separated from me**. I would have to **search for this part** for it would be the missing component I would need to accomplish my assignment.

Remember how we met without "knowing" too much about one another, but in twenty-eight days after meeting one another, we married? Well, the marriage began from obedience to God; however, the "knowing" came from the relationship with time. We would later know each other as we were known.

Two:

At the start of this chapter, I mentioned the definition and understanding of the word *wilderness*. I wrote that:
The original picture painted by this word to the Hebrews is "the arrangement of things to create order." The word *midvar* meaning *wilderness* is actually a place that exists as a perfectly arranged order as its ecosystem is in harmony and balance…God's will!

My relationship to my wife before time began was of oneness. This serves as a similitude of the exact oneness mankind had with God before the Fall. Once I started my earthly starting point (time) we were separated (enmity).

Nevertheless, I would have to find her like God had to find man (in time as we know it) because he (man) had fallen so deep into the abyss of sin. The focus here is not the sin, but that sin caused mankind to be at enmity (separated or apart) from their Creator; hence, God said, "…*Where art thou?*" (Genesis

3:9; KJV).

The wilderness is the plan for the relationship or to restore the relationship (bring us back to God) as it was in the beginning and before time. It is the ordered arrangement to create order in an unbalanced relationship. I too had to learn this in my own relationship with my wife to understand God in time. It was difficult because my wife did not know if I would love her or treat her children in a manner that she had previously experienced in relationships prior to meeting me, but it took time.

We desperately needed "the wilderness" as the order if we were to learn of God and each other. This is why Jesus said:

> "Take my yoke upon you, **and learn of me**; for I am meek and lowly in heart: and ye shall find rest unto your souls. For my yoke is easy, and my burden is light…" (Matthew 11:29, 30).

The learning benefits you and I, because what was unknown to us due to sin, we can now know of God through having a right relationship! Our marriage was and is that example labeled "wilderness" along with every twist and turn, every church visited, every pastor I met, and every experience you've read in our story. Our wilderness is that which drew us closer to God—like God had placed Israel in their environment and taught them balance, order and harmony. He had done the same with Stephanie and me; this is how we learned of Him.

It's what restored steadiness and agreement to a relationship started, but gone bad. What you've witnessed, my friend, was pages upon pages of stories of two people wandering in their wilderness, complete with complex maneuvering (spiritual guidance), the total wisdom of God, while gently and lovingly tolerating our total ignorance of Him. The immense time it took, given the years of heartache and pain endured by my wife and me, suggests and proves His endearing patience for His people.

Chapter 8: The Wilderness—The Sum Of All Things

Order

My relationship with my wife brought with it the order of God, and ultimately, the order of life. It was the catalyst by which many things hinged with predetermination and with purpose. This is the reason Scripture tells us: "For this reason a man will leave his father and mother and be united to his wife, and the two will become one flesh…" (Matthew 19:5).

The first man Adam illustrated this truth as God used him and his wife to establish a clear order. This is why it was vitally important that I be joined to the right person as it would bring me to the complete overall purpose that God wanted to accomplish in me as well as reestablish the order lost through sin. Every encounter experienced before I married was preparation for that moment. Everything I experienced afterward was to complete the maturing process relevant to a relationship to God through salvation through Christ and in marriage.

After I was joined together in marriage both to God and my wife, not only had the journey begun, but it had begun with a promise of God: "What therefore God hath joined together, let not man put asunder" (Mark 10:9). From this moment, I was no longer to know separation (enmity) again until death do us part, but now complete and joined with God.

Balance

Our experiences with every church brought with it a degree of balance.

Proverbs 11:1 states: "A false balance is abomination to the Lord: but a just weight is his delight" (KJV).

When carefully considering this passage of Scripture, its deeper mystery can be easily misinterpreted. So let's venture to apprehend that mystery while unlocking its powerful meaning.

We will start by discovering each word in order to exegete the text:

A false — "deceit, treachery"
Balance — This word is the Hebrew word mō·zān which means "scales, balance"; however, the root word (etymology and what we are after) is ä·zan' which means "to weigh, test, prove, consider."
Is abomination — "a disgusting thing, abomination, abominable"
To the Lord — Jehovah, "the existing One"
But a just — "complete, perfect, whole, full, at peace"
Weight — "precious stones, stones of fire"

The Word of God also suggests in 1 Peter 2:5, "You also, **like living stones**, are being built into a spiritual house to be a holy priesthood, offering spiritual sacrifices acceptable to God through Jesus Christ." We can conclude that God's view of us is, in a sense, as living stones, nonetheless stones!

Is his delight — "pleasure, delight, favor, goodwill, acceptance, will"

Now that we've compiled the evidence, let's review some key words from this passage and draw a conclusion relative to what I'm trying to convey! Every church involvement was, in fact, a twofold experience: 1) To bring balance in our marriage and our relationship to God, and 2) To bring balance and understanding to the misleading, incorrect and deceitful doctrine we were exposed to in many churches about God. This wrong doctrine was an **abomination** to the **Lord**, a disgusting thing.

The Hebrew meaning of *false* is "deceit." Not only had Stephanie and I been deceived by the worldview of marriage, but we were misled, deceived and challenged by unlearned Christians on what they thought church was and is. Ultimately, we found in error through our experiences with God.

Chapter 8: The Wilderness—The Sum Of All Things

The word *balance*, as I have stated, is from the root word: *ä•zan'* which means "to weigh, test, prove, consider." It's no wonder looking back that we now understand that although we were deceived, hurt and bruised, God considered this in testing us, weighing us, and proving us. We couldn't escape it! God used it to eventually cause us to be joined together and to meet the complete purpose that He had for our lives. These trials were very painful, however needful. Stephanie and I were weighed like precious stones being handled and dealt with, much to the delight of God declaring us just, or (complete), rendered fit for His use.

The maturing was for right relationship with God, "To know God through allowed suffering." If He was indeed good, we had to experience evil. As the Psalmist said in Psalm 119:71 (NIV): "It is good for me that I have been afflicted; that I may learn thy statutes." Simply put, it was finally for the right to do true kingdom ministry—after we understood order, balance and now harmony.

Harmony

My relationship with my wife and family, my experiences within church; and learning to deal with people in the church, pulpit or pew, brought total harmony with God. These three are essential to one's relationship to his or her Creator, thus the "wilderness" involvement.

The word *harmony* means "agreement; accord, harmonious relations, a consistent orderly or pleasing arrangement." At the beginning of this chapter, I explained the interesting contrast between Webster's version and the Hebrew version on *wilderness*.

The Hebrew version expressed that it pleased God in choosing the wilderness for Israel's wanderings; and that this was the arrangement of things to create order. Subsequently, the wilderness is actually a place chosen by God for His people—as a perfectly arranged way to bring order, harmony and balance. By placing Israel in that environment, He was teaching them, which is exactly what He did for Stephanie and me. If you will allow Him the same privilege, He'll do the same for you.

Conclusion

The man of God that I became and am is due to the maturing of God through the waiting. The culmination of such validates the call on my life and activates me in the right to operate and gives me the authority to function within the kingdom through humility, an attribute many Christians do not possess due to inadequate testing. (Contrary to popular opinion, seminary does not do this.) They simply choose not to complete the proving by God to produce the standard He requires of every believer.

These correctional, perfected experiences have even strengthened my wife; today she is more focused, patient, humble; and yet, she walks with boldness concerning the things of God. Through "Waiting on God," He has taught her the importance of her role as a wife, a mother, as well as her calling in ministry. Now with confidence as a team, we can operate in the fullness of God and His order with harmony and balance.

We have learned through the wilderness how to commune with God, and we are now equipped to operate, within His Excellency, wherever He sends us. Whether in church, music, entrepreneurship, writing, or business, we are perfected for the work of the kingdom of God. The qualifying mechanism of God demanded the real experience we were in. Therefore, elevation from God was the inescapable intent! This too was the Apostle Paul's experience: "the more excellent way!"

WAIT ON GOD!

ABOUT THE AUTHORS

Kevin L. Lipsey, Sr.
Kevin L. Lipsey, Sr., Preacher/Teacher/Author /Husband to Stephanie Lipsey/Father to four children, and native of Atlanta, Georgia.

This highly recognized leader, whose studies in theology, apologetics and world religion, have made him a sought-after authority within the body of Christ. Currently a shepherd for many, in this season God has positioned Kevin Lipsey, Sr., on assignment through KLMinistries, Inc. His purpose is to evangelize, teach and preach, bringing order to the body of Christ through love and correction. His purpose is to impart truth and transcend all denominations, bringing believers into maturity, and teaching the importance of waiting on God.

Stephanie S. Lipsey

Stephanie S. Lipsey, originally from Macon, Georgia, has lived in Atlanta since 1994. Married to Kevin Lipsey since 2000, she has embraced the many facets of ministry. During the years, she has assisted many women in their relationships as it pertains to marriage, children, and business. As a master cosmetologist, Stephanie uses her platform to give godly counsel as she helps women appreciate their beauty from the inside out. She enjoys helping others and is passionate about natural hair and wellness. In this season, she assists her husband in ministry and is the co-owner of a natural hair salon in Midtown, Atlanta. Stephanie and Kevin, together has a blended family of four wonderful children.

www.ingramcontent.com/pod-product-compliance
Lightning Source LLC
Chambersburg PA
CBHW031418290426
44110CB00011B/439